Woodworking

Step by Step Guide, DIY Plans & Projects Book

(Woodworking Tips, Techniques, Tools and their Creators)

Jack Mallory

Published By **Tyson Maxwell**

Jack Mallory

All Rights Reserved

Woodworking: Step by Step Guide, DIY Plans & Projects Book (Woodworking Tips, Techniques, Tools and their Creators)

ISBN 978-1-77485-620-8

No part of this guidebook shall be reproduced in any form without permission in writing from the publisher except in the case of brief quotations embodied in critical articles or reviews.

Legal & Disclaimer

The information contained in this ebook is not designed to replace or take the place of any form of medicine or professional medical advice. The information in this ebook has been provided for educational & entertainment purposes only.

The information contained in this book has been compiled from sources deemed reliable, and it is accurate to the best of the Author's knowledge; however, the Author cannot guarantee its accuracy and validity and cannot be held liable for any errors or omissions. Changes are periodically made to this book. You must consult your doctor or get professional medical advice before using any of the suggested remedies, techniques, or information in this book.

Upon using the information contained in this book, you agree to hold harmless the Author from and against any damages, costs, and expenses, including any legal fees potentially resulting from the application of any of the information provided by this guide. This disclaimer applies to any damages or injury caused by the use and application, whether directly or indirectly, of any advice or information presented, whether for breach of contract, tort, negligence, personal injury, criminal intent, or under any other cause of action.

You agree to accept all risks of using the information presented inside this book. You need to consult a professional medical practitioner in order to ensure you are both able and healthy enough to participate in this program.

Table of Contents

Chapter 1: Woodworking Central - Must Have Woodworking Tool............ 1

Chapter 2: How To Build And Install A Hall Table 15

Chapter 3: Wood.................................. 28

Chapter 4: Wood Work On The Lawn And Garden................................... 41

Chapter 5: Skill-Building Project............. 48

Chapter 6: Woodworking Security And Maintenance.......................... 63

Chapter 7: Basics Of Woodworking........ 81

Chapter 8: How To Grow Your Business Using The Chain Markets 95

Chapter 9: Coffee Mug Rack 105

Chapter 10: Stationary Tools................ 114

Chapter 11: The Woodworking Router (And Its Supporting Tool) 125

Chapter 12: How To Create Bracket Feet 136

Chapter 13: How To Construct Drafters 145

Chapter 14: The Use Of Specialized Metal Fasteners 152

Chapter 15: Safety Precautions For Woodworking 162

Conclusion 183

Chapter 1: Woodworking Central - Must Have Woodworking Tool

Just as in any other trade woodworking uses tools from another trade. To create quality products, craftsmen need the right tools. Tools for woodworking are not necessarily expensive or difficult. All that matters is your expertise and proper use of your tools. This chapter will focus on the basics tools that every woodworker must have.

1: Claw Hinge

The claw and the finished head must be well balanced. You will have trouble driving nails in nails if your claw hammer isn't balanced. You can either choose a wooden-handled hammer to reduce stress and strain on your wrists or a metallic handle harmer that has a rubberized grasp for added control and comfort. A 20 oz. A 20 oz. hammer works well for woodworking.

2: Tape Measures

Take a 25 foot retractable tape measurement. It'll be more difficult to roll it up if the tape is longer. It is important that you have a tab or a 'hook' at each end. Losse tabs or hooks will cause 1/8 inch measurement variations, which can lead to errors in accuracy. Accuracy problems could cause many issues in your work and/or lead to financial and time setbacks.

3: Utility Knives

Safety is paramount when knives have disposable blades that are retractable to the handle. A utility knife can be used for cutting wood and to clean out mortise joints.

4: Moisture Meter

Check the wood moisture content before you start any project. This will ensure that it is successful. Pin less meters have technology that resists the wood's surface moisture. Your meter should have different settings for different wood species.

5: Chisels

Chisels can also be used for woodcarving or cleaning out saw cuts. Certain chisels may be made of high-alloy or chromium carbon steel. Some also feature hardwood grips and metal caps for hammering. There are many sizes available for woodworking. 1/4" is used for mortise. 3/4" and 1" are used for door hinges. 1 1/2" is used for chipping away. A corner chisel can be used to cut notches.

Your chisels should fit your hand well. If you don't want to damage your chisel head, you can use a wooden tool or mallet. Keep your chisels in tip-top shape and oil the metal after every use.

You can prevent sharp edges from being damaged by placing edge caps over them or storing them in a roll or in a toolbox drawer. When working with a tool, use both your left and right hands. You can also bump the chisel using your free hand's heel. A claw hammer can continue to damage the chisel's end and eventually cause it to break.

To sharpen your tools, use stones instead of a grinding wheel. To file the blades properly, you will need a stone set that contains finer grit. You can start by sharpening the blades with a coarser quality, and then go on to finer grades. To get the best results, you can moisten your stone with oil. You should never sharpen the blades near your body.

6: Screwdrivers

Buy a variety. At the very least, you should have three types of screwdrivers: one large, one medium and one small one with a Philips head. Flat head screwdrivers also need to be kept in mind. The various sizes will make woodworking more fun and easier. I recommend you only use high-quality screwsdrivers. These can be used for many purposes and can be flattened when they are worn out. As much as possible, you should match the size of your head and the screw you're working on.

7: Nail sets

Buy several sizes and types of nail sets. These are used to drive nailheads into wood just below the surface. This allows for you to fill any gaps in the wood before staining it. This will give your woodwork a professional look.

8: Layout Square

A layout square can be purchased in either 6 or 12 inches sizes. Both are good options. However, the 6 in model is more user-friendly and portable. You can use the layout to mark out square cuts on wood or measure angles. Metal layouts squares are stronger, more accurate and last longer that plastic.

9: Clamps

I recommend having several clamps to fit 45- and 90 degree joints. C clamps are F clamps and M camps. All clamps that are required to complete your project should be owned or available.

Frame Jig

You should own at most a few of these jigs. A jig makes woodworking much more enjoyable if it is used properly. A jig helps you to stay on track and guide the tools in your project. You will use it to guide the pieces into a saw or to cut perfect circles. If you are making furniture with tapered feet, a tool like a Jig will help to not have to mark every angle. One example is the dovetail, which guides wood when making dovetail joints.

10 and11: Handsaws or Mitersaws

It is almost impossible to not own a few high quality handsaws. Handsaws can be used to do more detail work than a power saw. Handsaws allow for you to feel and see the chemistry between the blade of the saw and the wood. Drop and miter saws are just two of the handsaws you need.

12: Feather Board

A feather-board works well when pushing pieces beyond the cutting edge. It allows you to make smooth, high-quality cut. You can make your very own feather-board, or you can buy one.

13: Storage systems

Proper storage is something that I cannot stress enough. Properly storing and organizing your tools is crucial to the life and durability of your tools. Many tools can be costly so you should take good care. Many tools used in woodworking are very sharp. Incorrect storage or care can result not only in frustration but also serious injury. Don't leave any tools lying around. Don't let yourself be lazy. Take care of you workspace and your tools. This will give you the peace of head and safety that money can't buy. You can either place a pegboard for your hand tools next to your work bench or use a rolling mechanical's toolbox. Make sure you have a tackle container for all your fasteners. There are many options for bins that can be used to store the woodworking bits you accumulate. Bottom line is that proper storage is all about a S.Y.S.T.E.M (Save-Yourself-Stress-Time-Energy-and-Money).

14: Power Drills

The power drills are less expensive than cordless ones and can do more work. Power drills also have a wide range of uses and are easy to use. There are many different types and sizes of power drills. It all depends on what you need and how big or small you want it to be.

15: Table Saw

A Table Saw is your workhorse. Make sure to get a good one. It can be used for mitering, ripping, shaping, groove, square, joining, and other tasks. But you need to make sure that the tool is best suited for your specific needs. I recommend that you buy one with a tough work face that can withstand high-pressure woodworking projects. You will also need a handle for lifting and lowering the saw blade. Another handle can be used to adjust angle of the Table Saw blade. The Table Saw you select should have the power to cut through hard wood and make larger cuts. You should consider the motor's horsepower when you are looking to buy a Table Saw. The motor for your Table Saw must start smoothly with minimal vibration. To ensure your safety and that others are safe, your Table Saw must have a blade shield. Additionally, the on/off switches can be reached using a knee paddle.

Regular cleaning and maintenance is necessary for your Table Saw. Keep the area close to your saw blade free of pitch. To dissolve the pitch, you could soak your saws blades in oven cleaner. After that, use a non-abrasive to gently scrub the blades. Scrubbing cleaners can scratch your saw blades and decrease their durability. more pitch. To prolong its life, you can sharpen blades that are carbide.

You can get rust on your worktable so wipe it off after you have applied protection grease. You can also use a non-staining protectant such car wax on the Table Saw's top. You should avoid silicone wax because it can cause problems in the end.

16: Routers

A router is used in shaping the edges and corners of your work. It is available in various sizes, shapes, and bits. A stationery router is the best choice for someone starting out their woodworking journey. A router table might be necessary for those who already own a stationary router. A router table will allow you to make longer cuts in wood. A router with more horsepower (HP) than 2 will be easier for working with hardwoods. However, a variable speed router is more versatile and can help you avoid burning your bits.

A router can be made in 1/4" or 1/2 inch collet sizes. Although smaller bits can fit into larger collets, you cannot place larger ones into smaller collets. The switch to turn on or off your router should be reachable with just one finger.

17: A Jigsaw/ Sabre Saw

A jigsaw, or Sabre Saw, can be used to create intricate or simple patterns. It is important to choose an electric tool that is comfortable for your hand so you can have better control over the saw. Jigsaws should be used to cut softwood no greater than 1-1/2 in thick. A Jigsaw also has the ability to cut hardwood up until 3/4 inches thick. Jigsaw blades can bend if they are used to cut thicker boards. The Jigsaw blade can bend and leave a beveled instead of a square edge.

18: Band Saw

A band saw is one the most popular power tools in woodcarving. It's extremely useful for cutting scrap and other woodworking activities.

19. Circular saw

It is important to choose a high-quality circular saw when searching for one. This is an extremely useful power tool. A circular saw can have interchangeable blades which can be modified to fit your needs. The blades will cut your wood more evenly, but they are less smooth. Fine-toothed blades cut slowly and gather more dust. They are quicker and more durable, but also burn faster. Be sure to keep your saw blade collection varied. Also, remember that wood moisture can have an impact on your cuts.

20: Block Plane

A Block Plane allows for versatility in the execution of a project. To flatten or square pieces of wood, or to carve or shape your work, a block plane is a great tool. Block planes can be used to smoothen out dovetailed wood pieces. You should keep your Block Plane's blades sharp, as with all of your woodworking knives.

21: Workbench

This is your workspace. It is available in a variety options (portable, on wheels, or fixed). You need to select the worktable that is most appropriate for your woodworking requirements.

We have now covered all the tools and equipment required for woodworking. Let's look at advanced and basic woodworking techniques.

Chapter 2: How To Build And Install A Hall Table

As a student, I planned to make a dining table. Many of my classmates made furniture with legs that tapered from the bottom up to the top to echo the shape and feel of the flower. I gave each leg the appearance of a tapered leg and finished it off with gentle curves on both ends. To display these graceful shapes, I removed the table's corners and made the apron-faces. They were designed to fit the profile the legs. The table was made out of shedua and maple for the drawer sides as well as the bottom. This piece is fun to build. Although not as complex as a carcase item, the design goes beyond a simple table with drawers. This will help you develop as a woodworker. There are many ways to join wood, from traditional mortiseandtenon joints to dovetails. I also enjoy shaping legs and aprons. This is why I mix machine work with hand tools.

Begin by joining the joinery

* While the stock is still square, cut all the joinery.

* To join the narrow legs to the apron, I interlocked mortiseandtenon joints.

* I routed the mortises by hand and then cut the tenons with a tablesaw.

* Test the setups with sample material after you've cut the tenons. Set up a marking gauge and place each piece on the shoulder.

* For cutting the shoulders, clamp a stop onto a crosscutsled.

Cut the wide exteriors first. Then, adjust the blade until it is at the proper height for cutting the shoulder on the apron edges.

* Put a piece if blue tape around the stop to offset it.

* This will leave a small bit of extra material at the shoulder which can be cut flush.

* To cut the cheeks, I used a knife and a bandsaw to remove any remaining waste from the ends.

* Clean up, and then fit the joints using files and chisels.

* I have my tenons rounded instead of making the mortises square.

* After you have completed all the joinery, cut the drawer's front from the apron.

* Dry-fit the end components and measure the inside distances in the front and back aprons to determine length of the interiorrails.

* Take this measurement as close as your legs to ensure the highest accuracy.

How to make your drawer pocket

* The drawer enclosure consists of a pair or interior rails. They are each narrower that the aprons running front to back, and help guide the drawer sides.

* The rails are joined by dowels to their front and rear ends.

* This panel closes the compartment and adds rigidity. It also supports the drawer from beneath.

* Interior rails must be parallel and have dowel joints aligned front to rear to allow smooth drawer movement.

* I used the front Aprons to help me accurately lay out the joints for the rear apron.

* A doweling jig, I made my holes with a shopmade doweling jig.

* To drill the front apron for drilling, position the jig to ensure its reference face is aligned with the apron's internal edge.

* While you attach the jig to your work surface temporarily, fasten it with a few brads.

* On the drill press, set the bit depth.

* Place your layout markings on the drill bit.

* Position the jig at the end of the corresponding rail after drilling the pron.

* Repeat the above process with all the aprons and rail ends.

* Make sure all holes are dug.

* A way to reduce the time it takes to test dowel joints is to only utalize them in half of the holes.

* Also, it helps to compress them by rolling in the file and placing them on your bench.

* Multiple dry fits keep the dowel holes tight.

How to build and attach the panel and frame

* The bottom panel of the drawer pocket is a piece of plywood that has been glued to a frame with bridle joints.

* These joints are simple to cut with a tablesaw and tenoning Jig. The glue is thick enough to make them very sturdy.

* As the drawer runs directly over the frame, the joinery was oriented so the grain is unbroken from front and back.

* I made this frame wider so I could handplane it to the right fit.

* To conceal the end grain at the frame's edge, I added 1/8 inches of edge-banding.

* While the panel is not visible, it is important to note that the frame has a panel for beauty rather than strength.

* Use primary venture wood for utalization, and care in assembling the pieces.

* I cut the tongue from the panel, as well as the stopped grooves which hold it, using a router table with fence and straight bit.

* Sand the panel before you do this step.

* Afterward, you may need to sand the area a lot.

* Prefinish the panel, as well the frame's inside edges.

* Once glue has dried, cut 1/8 inch off the front edge.

* Clean the edge-banding, then plane the edges to achieve the desired fit.

Shaping

* Once all joinery pieces have been cut and fitted, the shaping process can begin.

* I fashioned the outside face of each leg in an elongated taper, which ends in a graceful curve at top.

* I also made sure that the taper of each leg's legs was followed by the face for consistency.

* Last, I made a slight bevel in the top to match it with the rest.

* Place a bandsaw next to one of the template layout lines.

* Lay the template on top of the bandsawn outer and then draw a new line for cutting adjacent faces.

* Use a combination (block and smoothing, scraper, sandpaper) to work the curves out and smooth the exteriors.

* The taper around the apron's face is subtle and just a hand-planed adjustment.

* To create the taper, dryfit each legand apron connection.

* Place a mark at this point along the bottom of the apron, and connect it with the top edge.

* This pair guides the planing.

* I used an angled block plane to chamfer the top edges and bottom of each leg to prevent chipping.

* I also used both a block and spoke plane to make a subtle curve along the bottom edge of each Apron.

* Dry-fit the tables to ensure uniform tapers.

* The cut-out distance between the legs should not be too large and consistent so that the top can expand or contract.

Finishing

* I almost always prefinish any piece before glue-up.

* It's very easy to put a brush and pad in tight places once you have separated the parts.

* The result is extremely uniform, even if the wax and shellac are applied in multiple layers.

* Prep by sanding and breaking down edges to obtain P400 grit. Take special care to the end grain.

* Tape off any exteriors which may be affected by glue.

* Gluing up pieces with many parts can lead to a mad dash to attach glue to the various exteriors, then clamp the joints and get them together before the parts start seizing.

* I have broken the process down into four manageable stages for greater control.

* Connect the two side pieces together and clamp them.

* If you have those in clamps, there is plenty of time to glue dowels into drawer rails' ends.

* Once glue has dried, glue drawer rails into front and rear Aprons.

* Once you have the assembly assembled, dryfit into the legs.

* Once glue is dry, you can remove the leg assemblies by unclamping them.

* Apply glue to both the front and back aprons, secure them in their mortises, clamp, and

* Once the clamps are removed, glue the bottom frame-and-panel into its rabbets.

After the base has been completed, trim and fit the drawer joints.

* Assemble your drawer, following the contour of its bottom edge.

* After the drawer is glued up shape the front and bottom edges to match the Aprons.

* Turn the drawer so that it is fully in the drawer pocket.

* Use sharp pencils to draw the outline from the drawer's front rail to the end grains.

* Remember to mark both sides.

* Plane closer to the lines

* Check the drawer pocket regularly to see the final shape as you work.

* There are many methods to fasten the top of the table to the base.

* I used handmade brass brackets. But, you could also use commercially made figure eights.

* Remove the fasteners from the recess.

* Attach the brackets first to the aprons. Next, attach the top.

Chapter 3: Wood

Wood is the basis of all woodworking. The art and craft of woodworking is, as the name suggests. It's all about working in wood. This is the wood. Being a woodworker would be a good investment. You'll find the "knowing your wood" section a bit later in the book. Here you will learn about different wood qualities and how to adapt as a qualified Woodworker. This chapter will focus on exotic, hardwood and softwood. It will also discuss the differences and the many wood types that are included in each of these categories. This chapter will also talk about where to buy woods.

Hard Wood

Hardwoods come from angiosperm-trees. Angiosperm can be used to describe trees that are able to grow normal leaves and produce seeds. Contrary some belief hardwood is not harder or softer than hardwood. Some hardwoods have a strong structure that makes them easier and more stable for use, while others are less sturdy. This section covers some common hardwood types such as maple and mahogany.

Common hardwood

Ash

This hardwood can be found in shades of white or pale brown. It has a straight, straight grain. It is becoming more rare than most hardwoods but still very accessible. It is known for its superior stain resistance and can be used as a substitute for white oak in many instances.

Birch

Birch is a common hardwood. It can be found in two colors, yellow and white.

Yellow birch is available in shades between white and yellow while its central shade takes on a reddish to brown hue. White birch is a lighter color and can often be mistaken for maple. Birch is known for its hardiness and stability. Unfortunately, it can be very difficult to stain. Birch wood tends to produce uneven results, so it's best to keep products made with birch wood painted.

Cherry

Cherry wood, which is a darker shade than white with a reddishbrown central, is another very popular type of hardwood. The cherry wood is very popular, and it is also easy to get, despite the increasing price due to high demand. Its many positive qualities are what make it so popular. It has all the characteristics that a woodworker would want. It isn't painful to work on, easy to stain with ordinary oil, and it also finishes well. This hardwood scored 2 on a scale of 1-5 for hardness. On a scale from 1 to 5, the cherry wood was rated 2 in hardness.

Mahogany

The hardness 2 of mahogany is between the ratings 1 and 5. This wood, like the cherrywoods, is excellent for furniture making. It is also called Honduran mahogany. This wood is available in several shades, including reddish-brown or deep red. It is as strong as cherry when it comes to resisting stains. You can finish it with one to ten oil layers. Mahogany is in danger of disappearing completely due to its rarity and deforestation. It will be very expensive when it is recovered.

Maple

Maple is a hardwood that is known for being stable and strong. Maple is a hard wood. It is rated 5 by using a 1-5 scale to measure its hardness. It makes it difficult for woodworkers. There are two types: hard and soft maple. While hard maple is more difficult to mine, soft maple tends to be easier.

Oak

This wood is another well-known one, especially for furniture making. It is strong and can withstand a range of temperatures from 1 to 5. Oak is available in two major types, which are classified according to their appearance - red oak and white oak. While both types of oak can be found, the availability of white oak is greater than that for red oak. You can usually find white oak only at the lumberyard. White oak is also used to make furniture that will withstand water and be outdoors. White oak is resistant to high moisture and can be used outdoors without any major damage. It is also more attractive due to the ray-flaked patterns of its grains. White oak is highly sought after, especially for furniture manufacturing.

It is also worth noting, that white oak is usually more affordable than other hardwoods. This is especially true if the wood is quarter sawn.

Poplar

Popular is also a popular hardwood. It has a less-than-pleasing appearance. To make it more pleasing to the eyes, almost every hardwood is painted. It has a 1 rating for its hardness. The range is from 1 to 5, which indicates its softness. Poplar is a white wood with streaks in the brown or green shades. Poplar has a less pleasing appearance and is rarely used for furniture making.

Softwoods

Coniferous woods are used to make softwoods. Coniferous forests are the literal name given to gymnosperms. The modified leaves of softwood trees, which have needle-like forms and produce cones, are the key characteristics. It is incorrect for coniferous hardwoods to be called softwoods, as they are "softer" and weaker than hardwoods. Many kinds of softwoods are stronger than hardwoods. Redwood, Pine and Cedar are all common softwoods. Some of these are listed below.

Common softwoods

Cedar

Cedar is a commonly used softwood. It's used in furniture production for both indoor and exterior purposes. Cedarwood is naturally resistant to moths. This is one of its many advantages. Cedarwood is often used to create chests, closets, or similar structures that house clothes or vulnerable items. Cedar wood is also highly prized for its strength, which is why it's so widely used in woodwork. It is also very strong. It can be used to build protection systems, such as wood shingles. Wood shingles are pieces made of wood that have a narrowed end. They can protect the walls and roofs of houses from extreme weather conditions.

Cedar is also resistant to distortions, such as cracking or warping. This makes cedar well-suited for woodworking. This quality makes cedar a suitable candidate for indoor panels for rooms in the house.

The Western Red Cedar, a common form of cedar, is actually not the genuine cedar. Red, the Western Red Cedar can be rated 1 in softness. This cedar tree is used in the construction of outdoor creations. These creations include decks or other furniture. This is because it can withstand water in the environment and doesn't get damaged.

In addition to these wonderful qualities, the great news is cedar, particularly Western Red Cedar can be easily found at your local hardware store.

Redwood

Another type of softwood commonly used in woodwork are redwood and spruce. Similar to cedar it is resistant to moisture-induced rot. It is widely used outdoors. As you can guess from the name, it's red. It also has a grading level of 2 in softness on a scale between 1 and 5. It is very easy to work with, and it doesn't cost much. Redwood is easily found in your closest hardware store.

Pine

Pine is one of most widely-used woods in the building, carpentry, allied ventures, and construction industries. It is used in windows and as flooring in many homes. Its smooth, elegant and beautiful grain is one of the reasons. Pine woods have beautiful knots. They are tidy and lend a project a refined appearance. It is amazing to note that some pine varieties are one of nature's strongest softwoods. These woods are also popular with woodworkers and other manufacturers. The main forms of pine wood are white, sugary, yellows, and Ponderosa.

It is also difficult to work with Pine because of its soft varieties. While it does not make staining impossible it must be sealed first. However, Ponderosas are known to secrete sap. One must be mindful of this.

Pine can be found at your local hardware stores, though it is likely to be of lesser quality than what you would find at a lumberyard.

Fir

This softwood is used in building construction. It shows a straight grain. It has a reddish to brown hue. Its grain pattern doesn't look very beautiful but it is used to make furniture. It can be disappointing when it comes time to apply stain. Therefore, painting is a better option. Douglas fir also goes by the name Fir. This wood is strong for softwood. It is rated at 4 out 4 in terms strength. This wood is inexpensive, so you can save your money.

Exotic Woods

The term exotic wood can be used to describe woods that aren't available in North America. Exotic woods can be woods whose tree varieties are not the native species. Mahogany, bamboo, Brazilian cherry and other exotic woods are some examples. The texture and appearance of exotic woods is different from their native species. People might choose exotic species for its roughness and appearance compared to native-grown trees. Domestic wood is the antithesis of exotic timber. Domestic wood can be used to refer to woods that were grown in their natural environment.

There are other reasons that people may choose to purchase exotic woods over domestic woods. You might value the exotic wood's "modern air" and support local wood-related activities. Exotic woods can be more costly than native counterparts that have approximately the same features.

Sources for purchasing wood

* Superstores near you

* The closest lumberyard

* You can order by phone or postal mail

* Home wood depot

* Etsy

* Architectural salvage retailers

* Local demolition sites

Chapter 4: Wood Work On The Lawn And Garden

Your lawn or garden should be the only part of your residence that allows you to relax and have some rest. It should be where you go to get away from the stress and bustle. To enhance the relaxation, rest and laid-back atmosphere of your lawn and garden, you can use these woodworking ideas.

Wooden Doormat

You don't want to be a sloppy doormat if there's a lot going on in your house. It is important that you have somewhere to wipe the dirt, grass, or potting soil from your feet after you've spent a day out in the garden.

This is where wooden doormats come in. Take out your tape measurer and attach the tape to the desired wooden material to make your own wooden floor mat. Take measurements to determine the dimensions of your doormat. These dimensions are entirely up to the user, so do what works.

You can now use a crayon or black marker for marking the areas where you should make your first cuts on the wooden surface. After you have completed this step, you can get your hand drill out and begin drilling holes to make your wooden doormat.

Next, smoothen any rough edges with your power jointer by running your wooden floormat across it. You can then focus on the aesthetics of your wooden doormat. If you want your doormat to look even better, you can paint a good-looking wood stain on it. It is then time to let the mat dry in the sun outside.

Wooden Garden Stool

You can take a seat in the garden, but it is best to be careful what you use as a chair. I used enjoy sitting on a stump in my yard until I was attacked by a bunch wild fire ants. A wooden garden stool is a better option to avoid such a fate. Even if all the earth isn't your home, you can still make it your footstool by making the garden yours!

Requisition the major parts of the stool to begin the construction process. This is where you will create your seat, legs, and bracingboards. For this project, you will need four 5 inch bracing boards and four 5 in. long legs. You also need a 2 by 4in seat. This is how you will build your garden stool. These pieces will support your stool's base structure.

Double-check and use your tape measuring device to confirm that you got it right. After you have determined the dimensions, you will be able to use standard nailing for attaching your legs on to your bracing. Now you can place your seat using woodworking glue. The Wooden Garden Stool can be placed in the sun and left to dry.

Making raised garden beds

Although designing raised garden beds is very simple, it will save you time and effort in the end. For the first step, you will need four 4 x 4, 5 foot long pieces of 4 x 4. These should be placed in the borders to your garden. As you can see, the shape should be rectangular.

This is your garden's framework. It doesn't have be very specific. It doesn't matter what size your garden is. Your garden bed frame can be adjusted so that it matches your garden. Simply top it with a headpiece measuring approximately 6 inches and a bottomboard measuring 4 inches. Once you are happy with your garden beds, make a drainage ditch 3 feet long in the back.

Cold Frames

If you enjoy gardening and want to extend the growing season through winter, then it would be worthwhile to embark on a woodworking task of building a coldframe. Cold frames combine the best aspects of woodworking with gardening. They are both practical and entertaining. They are extremely simple to make.

These items function as tiny greenhouses. The little sun that is available during winter months can focus and filter down to the crops planted within the frame. It is easy to construct. You simply need four 2x4s to assemble into a rectangular shape over any plants you wish.

After this is done, you can take a piece of plastic or tarp off the frame and wrap it around the plants. The edges of the plastic material should be secured to the wood. This will prevent it from being damaged. That's all folks! Your garden's life expectancy can be greatly increased by using some woodworking skills! Enjoy!

Constructing compost containers

To ensure your garden is successful, the material we call "compost", is crucial. It's just as important to make sure the compost does what it is meant to do. How do I make a compost-bin? That's easy. Take a look at it. Dig four equal-sized holes into a square in a garden spot.

When I refer to "free", I mean an area free of plants and other obstructions. After you have completed this, obtain four 2x4-inch pieces wood for each hole. These 2x4's must be submerged in the ground at least 4 feet to make them work.

Once you've done all of this, you'll want to grab some strong 2x2's and use them for filling in the spaces between your two x four wooden posts. These are the walls that will make up your compost bin. You can use them to fill each side of your walled-in posts. When you are done, you should be left with a large wooden frame in your yard. Now add compost to this box and you're ready to go!

Planter Box

These beautifully crafted wood planter boxes work well in your garden. Conifer is a good choice of softwood materials to build your own. You will need to create a base and top, trim, sides, and any optional lattice.

Carbon paper can be used to create these dimensions. Next, run your wood through your power saw and use your trusty handheld saw to cut them. These pieces can then be assembled using wood screws, glue or just by drilling into the joints.

Chapter 5: Skill-Building Project

PLANK HEADBOARD

Getting Started This cut-list provides sizes for all other sizes.

Select straight wood. If you want to add some character, consider boards that are rustic, with cracks and knots, but still straight. A lumber store can be organized according to the cutlist, which will save you time and money. Use safety goggles to protect your eyes and provide ventilation for painting.

Assemble one foot.

Put glue on at the very least one side 1x2 of the leg pieces. Lay 1x2,1x3 over the leg piece. Place the top edge of 1x2 downwards. The ends should be facing towards the glue. Every 6-8 inches, nail 1x2 or 1x3 using 1-1 to 1-1/4-inch nails. As you have seen, construct the legs as shown. Tip. Adjust the panels to flush your edges after you nail the board down.

Attach panel boards beginning at the headboard's highest position, then glue to the ends. Lay a 1x4 panels board on top of the feet. Attach 1-1/4-inch nails to the sides. Each panel board should be painted above the feet. Refer to pattern above for panels to be used as legs. Tip. Use a chisel and clash panel boards to give your headboard a rustic appearance.

Attach leg pieces

Apply glue to one side at least of two 1x3-inch leg pieces. Place them on the headboard legs, as shown in the illustration. Use 2 inch nails to attach the door's top edge and exterior edges.

Attach the Panel Trim the headboard by adhering glue to 1x4 panel trim boards and the panel cutting board to the tops of each headboard. Use 1-1/4-inch nails to attach the panel trim board and panel trimming board. Keep the outside edges flush.

Attach the trim to outside. Attach the trim headboard. (Minimum nails will appear at the front). Apply glue and then leave two nail pieces on each side of the foot. There may be slight excess material at the rear. Use 2-inch nails at 6-8 inches.

Attach the top trim

Apply glue at the headboard's top. Line leg trimming every 6-8 inches, with outer leg grinds or nail downs.

Keep straight in front of and around the doors edges.

Attach the headboards by applying glue to the top. Lift the headboard and attach it to the headboard by lifting the headboard up.

Tip for a king-size headboard: Use scrap wood to cut and then hold vertically with planks.

Finish the headboard

Wood filler should be used to plug the nail holes. Dry the sand. Next, sand again with 80-grit. Fill in any gaps. Wood filler can shrink as it dries. Sand again this point using 120-grit. Finally, sand the final point with 150-grit Sandpaper.

You can vacuum the headboard with a soft bristle brush attachment. Then, wipe the surface using a damp towel to remove any sanding residue. Apply a primer spray to the headboard, in accordance with the instructions. Let dry completely.

Work towards the wood grain by applying paint. Two coats of paint should be applied, giving each coat time to dry fully. Sandpaper can be used to distress the edges. To show cracks between panels, chisel between plankboards. Apply glaze to hazardous areas and wipe down until desired result is achieved. Spray the clear coat on your headboard to seal it.

Attach to the Frame

Stained Headboard: There are many options

I want to build the headboard. By using a stained finish, solid wood's beauty can be preserved. This headboard was finished with two coats in walnut oil-based stain. It was then coated with satin oil-based epoxy.

BEDSIDE TAPER

Contemporary Style Bedside Desk

Tools & Material:

* 3/4 "Meranti Plywood, an exotic hardwood of the Philippines

* 3/4" Solid Poplar

* 1/2" Prefinished Maple Plywood

* 18" Extended Dried Glider

* Braid With 2 / 8 "Braid Nails & 1-3/8 "pin Nails

* Power drill for 1" wood screws, 1-1 / 2, and 2-1/2 inch wood screws

* Addition of bit

* Pocket Jig

* Sandpaper/sander

* paint, polyurethane and other painting supplies

* Wood glue and wood putty

* I saw a Myrna, and a Table.

* Tape Measure

* Safety glasses

Steps:

Make the cupboard box from 3/4'solid Poplar. Use a table to cut the pieces.

- Top: 19-1 / 4 "x 36"

- two sides pieces: 19-1/ 4 "x 221-1/ 4"

- inner shelf and bottom section: 18- 1/2" x 2

34-1 /- back: 21-1 / 4 "x 36"

Use wood glue to attach the top, shelves and sides to your back. You should set the inner frame between 8-7 / 8 inches high. Then, attach the rock bottom shelf 1 in from the rock top.

Use 1/2 inch of maple to build two drawers boxes. See the table and then cut to size.

- Two-drawer Bottles: 17"x32-1/2 "

- Four drawers Backs & Fronts: 8 x 32-1 / 2.

- Four Drawer Sides: 18 "x 8

Assembled drawer containers. Make a half-Dado of rock bottom on the inside. Slide the rock top drawer piece into a dado groove.

One or two pieces (x 36") and 4-1/4" x36 (".

Attach two pieces of Poplar (glue to the center 1 inch Meranti 5 inches) at each end and long nails. A part of 1-inch is then attached with 4-1 glue and nails.

Use the wood putty for filling in nail holes. Then sand the surfaces. Allow to dry.

With glue and braided nails, attach the drawers fronts to your drawer box. Do it. Acts should not be moved. Rock bottom. Wood screws can be used for additional support to secure the actions inside the drawers to the drone.

WOODWINDOW WALLOW VALANCE

A house can be bought, but buying a home that is in need of repair and maintenance can be an entirely different story. I have been able to DIY all the furniture and decoration in my house through this method. Natural light is an important feature of my home that I enjoy. I also have three large, and three smaller, windows. Which leads me to today's post-- Wood Window Valance Tutorial!

These valances not only can beautify your windows, but also the whole living space. They can be bought for as little as $20!

Supply

1-inch x 2-inch x 12-foot (I used cedarwood) in the wood I chose

wood stain: I am a walnut slicing-sawdust user (I had one already so it wasn't an issue of price). If you don't have one. Ask someone who is a fan of saws or ask Lowe to cut wood for your needs.

* 1 inch wooden

* 2 2 1/2-inch wooden screws

* Metal corner bracket

* paintbrush, rag

* Sheer curtains are optional (mine was found at TJ Maxx and cost $ 10!)).

Your wood should be cut

I would love to know how you cut wood. ">1" Every window has its own unique characteristics, so your one touch will be different. I will list my dimensions and you will make your scale accordingly. Important note: After you confirm that your windows should be cut to 10-12 inches in length, don't allow the wooden window to touch the window. Instead, frame it.

For example, my sliding-glass door is 6ft in width. But I have made the length for my wood 7ft long, so it will be possible to extend more than 6 inches on each side.

Here are the measurements I used for my three large window.

Measurements

I have my two 7-foot windows, one 8-foot piece plus two 6-inch pieces. And two 4-inch sections.

Two 7-foot pieces, two 6-inch pieces and two 4-inch parts are needed for my 6-foot sliding-glass doors. Your first task is to cut all your wood. As I said, your measurements will differ from those I listed. Your life expectancy was twice confirmed. I used the saw to make cuts. Please exercise caution and take safety measures.

Once you are done, ensure that you have checked the edges before you start cutting.

In the end, you will need five pieces to make a single valence. Please don't be above me.

I was smudging it. I chose a pleasant dark brown wood stain. You can also choose a lighter or flowing brown depending on the decor.

Use a cotton pad or brush to stain the wood. A meeting can be messy, so I used that. The stain can be used in a large amount. Begin by dipping your brush and wiping off any excess. It will be almost impossible to find a dark piece of wood if it is not stained.

It's possible to paint large pieces of horseshoes with stain, then let them dry.

Assembly

Next is the assembly. To attach your 6 inch and 4 inch pieces to the corner of the wooden frame, use corner brackets. Do not worry about hanging the windows.

Use the included screws for corner brackets. These are used to attach the wood to a corner. You can check to make sure the surface edges are flush.

It is natural to think that we are going on to attach a substantial piece, but in reality we are just drilling pilot holes.

Place your larger piece on top the corner pieces (this can be useful for any participant). To ensure that your outer edges line up correctly, you will drill two pilot holes one at each end.

Scenes

Many creative Thanks to linking to add scenes to if you would like that option. To hold your curtains inside the Valence, you can use a tensionrod (such as a bath curtain). However, I found that large windows such my own make it difficult to find rods 7-8 feet in length. If you do find one, they will be quite expensive.

I chose to use simple brackets for curtains, especially smaller ones, as I want my curtains to only have decorative accents for wooden windows and not to close completely.

Make sure to grab your curtain before we hang the entire Valence. It is difficult to urge them otherwise.

Placement is everything. Make sure you connect the corners of your wall to your corner. As a guideline, use the edge of your window to align.

Attach the wooden corners of your valance to the wall with the two 1/2-inch screws. If you have trouble confirming the use of a wall anchor to attach your valance, then locate a stud where you can apply the screw.

You will have to add one corner to the mag-posh at the opposite side, but continue to verify and use a level in order to make sure it is not becoming unilateral.

You will need a partner to complete the final step. You can have your partner hold one end and pilot you through the hole. Attach the opposite side of the long wooden canyon to your 1-inch screws.

A farmhouse wooden window. You get a lot of value. These windows could be compared to 1,000,000 reindeer. However, they were only a few dollars to build.

Once the sand is dry, cover the screws using a touch-wood putty. Finally, add a little stain to hide the screws.

Chapter 6: Woodworking Security And Maintenance

Take safety measures

Safety is a key concern in woodworking. It does not matter if you are a beginner or a skilled woodworker, it is crucial to ensure safety when designing. Protection is essential for everyone around you. Working together in a woodworking store will ensure that everyone is healthy and happy.

The hazards of woodworking include sharp blades, parts and offensive power tools. It is common to be in a workshop where environmental threats, such as glues/paints and bits of sawdust can increase. However, there is always the risk of being shocked by an electric current or having your tools cut. The risk of being caught between running machine's running wheels by loose clothes, or hanging jewels is another possibility.

There are some benefits to woodworking. Woodworking is a wonderful hobby or profession that requires you to be aware of the dangers and be mindful of the climate. This is a great safety measure because you will be exposed to heavy machines and the tools. Working safely can be fun for hours, so it's worth the effort to learn simple safety rules.

You shouldn't let your workshop become a place to be careless or ignore safety rules. The keys to being safe in a woodworking workshop are knowledge and compliance. Protection requires more than just diligence. It takes dedication to ensure safety when working with the equipment. It is important to continue learning about safety protocols. Here are some woodworking safety tips.

1. Look Your Best

Appropriate clothing is also required for personal protection. The dress code you use for woodworking should stipulate that no clothing in the shop poses a risk. Lose, baggy clothing is the worst for transporting equipment.

Although you don't want to get too hot and itchy, you'll still need something comfy and not restrictive. You'll be more comfortable in long-sleeved shirts than T-shirts. Protection gear means wearing gloves under the appropriate circumstances. Comfortable shoes are also important.

2. Avoid Wearing Jewelry

Dangling chains or pendants made of wood are not appropriate for shops that specialize in woodworking. They are also more likely to catch moving blades, or spin straps. It can lead to life-threatening injuries if a neckchain or lanyard is caught in a handle.

It is important to protect it from damage if you have a valuable piece of jewelry. Put lanyards and tuck chain out of reach. You should also decide whether the ring on your ring finger or the watch you wear in your shop is safe. If you have even the slightest doubt, take it off.

3. Always wear safety glasses.

It will be very difficult to work with woodworking tools if you lose your vision. It will also be difficult to function without the use of your fingertips, toes, and toes. Every part of the body in a shop for woodworking poses a risk. Protective equipment or PPE (personal protective equipment) is the best way to stay safe.

Protection eyewear should have regular woodworking protection equipment. This could include safety glasses, side or full face shields, depending on the situation. OSHA standards must be met when your eyewear is worn. An insufficient investment can lead to poor eye security.

Include hearing protection and respiratory protection with your PPE kit. Ear protection comes in many forms, such as earmuffs or earplugs. Your work-related respirators should be included. It is possible to use a disposable dust shield when cutting timber. If you need to handle poisonous gases, you may also need a HEPA Filter.

4. You shouldn't alter bits or change blades when you use mechanines.

It is very dangerous to service any machine piece or power tool which is already energized. If you are using your running tool as a tool, make sure it has a plug-in power source. If a tool is being used for running, it will just wait to run out of power. When changing blades or parts, this is the time when you should be cautious.

It is important to ensure that when you swap out blades the instrument doesn't shut off with one click. Do not unplug any instrument's primary wire. You can also lock off the electricity to make yourself extra careful. However, it doesn't matter how you do this, make sure you have completely de-energized it before you start servicing it.

5. Avoid the use or abuse of alcohol and drugs

This tip should be ignored. It is astonishing, however how disabled people will forget their judgments and take up woodworking projects. This reckless decision could cause serious injury.

It is dangerous and irresponsible to drink alcohol while you are woodworking. They can change your mental state and make you more likely to use recreational drugs such as marijuana. You can get legal prescription pills that will help you quit, including anti-depressants as well as painkillers. Woodworking cannot be combined with any disability.

6. Sharp blades or bits recommended

While it seems risky, sharp blades make cutting easier. Broken, worn-out, blunt or scratched blades are dangerous. Sharp blades cut wood easily and leave behind a few sharp edges that can impale. These have fewer setbacks than the more risky aspects of woodworking.

For drill bits with sharp edges, it is the exact same. You won't get jammed or binded if your bits are dull or broken. The investment in high-quality blades and parts is well worth it. Your blades and bits should be sharpened by professionals.

Your cutting tools should never become dull.

7. Use wood to make nails

Reclaimed wood, which is extremely sought-after, is one of the best. It has a certain appeal that many people enjoy. Woodworkers should be aware that there are dangers lurking in old wood.

You should still inspect the wood for nail or other fasteners, before you begin to use it. Visual checks and telltale cracks can help you find embedded nails. It is best to use a metal detector for those who work with recycled wood. Don't let them damage your saw blades, or cause an accident. Grab any old nails regardless of what system you have.

8. Work against the Cutter

An experienced woodworker knows how work against the cutter. It's important to hold the work in front of the cutting instrument whenever possible. It's safer to force the work onto the work surface than to feed it against a stationary cutting blade. By working against the cutter, you can minimize the danger of a dangerous kickback.

This important safety tip is often overlooked by inexperienced woodworkers, hobbyists, and others. They've never used the tool to protect the cutter before. It's not obvious and isn't common. The next time you go to your shop, focus on your cutting tool.

9. Never Touch a Moving Knife More

Wait until a spinning blade stops spinning before touching it to remove waste, cut-offs or other debris. Before touching it. A push stick or a bit more debris can be used to keep it from falling apart.

10. Limit Distractions

It is frustrating to be continually or unexpectedly interrupted at work. Distractions distract you from what's important and force your attention to other things. Distractions can cause your hands and fingers to become weak and exposed.

In many ways, disturbances can arrive. This is usually someone who unofficially visits the shop. It can also come from outside sources, like radio programs or cars making noise. It is one of today's most distracting tools. For safety reasons, it is best to leave your cellphone in a quiet area.

Keep Your Workshop Clean

It is more pleasant to work in an organized environment. Your work area should be clean and tidy regardless of whether it's a garage for homeowners or an outside workshop for woodworkers. Just like your house, make sure that your workspace is clear and tidy.

Keep in mind that safety compliance is easier when there are no sharp edges or bent objects. Maintaining accurate inventory records, especially for small objects that may get lost due to sawdust. Customer retention increases, good ventilation improves personal health and hygiene.

There are many different ways to keep your workshop orderly. Let's go over a few ideas that worked well for us.

1. Create the right workshop design at the beginning.

When designing a workspace for your business, you need to consider how best to arrange the required equipment. You will need to determine the number of machines required and any other accessories for the workshop. It Is important to be imaginative when assembling the equipment. You should keep in mind that you will need to store timber and finished goods separately. To ensure that your woodwork is dust-free, you will need a dust collector and a suitable drainage system.

2. De-cluttering your shop

After a while, the workshop may start to get clogged up with old and duplicate equipment. It can make it more difficult to clean the shop and cause it to get clogged. You can then take stock of your shop and determine what you need. You can donate or keep valuable items in a separate space until you need them.

3. You should properly store your tools

First, ensure that you consider the safety of each piece. Some might not be suitable. Exposure to the air can cause machinery to rust. Some machines may require storage in drawers or boxes. This will ensure that your tools are preserved and you don't have to spend as much. Additionally, your workshop will look cleaner and more organized.

4. Vacuum and sweep frequently

You'll always have lots of sawdust to deal with in project management. Make sure to sweep the floor often to prevent dust accumulations. Regular vacuuming is a good idea to get rid of tiny allergens. These cleaning techniques ensure an allergy-free atmosphere.

5. Engage cleaning service

Woodworkers are always occupied with many tasks. You may find that cleaning is a large part of your day, which will affect your productivity. You'll have more time for creativity if you work with a cleaning agency/service that can do both the washing, trash, and recycling.

6. Get a tool organizer

Do you like having your tools organized and easily accessible? This is why you need a tool organizer. It can store smaller items, like hands, nails, and power tool, in one place. You can make it your own or adapt it to match an item.

7. Organize tools depending on projects

Do you have an important project on the horizon? In the workshop you will have to consider what you actually need. Each project has its own tools. It is best that you get rid of any unnecessary items. Moving around will make your life easier and leave you with a clear workspace.

8. Use cord management

In many workshops, the security of electrical, electronic, or other equipment cables seems like an afterthought. Cables invite dust to build up, which can cause you to sneeze. Unsecured cable can cause accidents and lead to injury. To keep your workplace cleaner, more efficient, and healthier, the cable manager must lift wires off the floor.

The tools you need for cleaning your workshop efficiently

* A Broom

* Dustpan

* Automatic floor scrubber

* Vacuum Cleaner

* Squeegee

* Towels

* Mop

Spray Bottle

How to conduct regular repair and maintenance of woodwork tools

It is essential to have great tools for woodworking that allow carpenters and other woodworkers be able to perform their jobs efficiently and in a reasonable time. When the letter is followed up with the maintenance and repair of the tools, efficiency and effectiveness in woodworking can only be achieved. Here are some tips for repairing your workshop.

1. Regular sharpening

Wooden chisels is one of the larger woodworking tools that needs to be regularly sharpened. Most of the tools used in woodworking are used for either drilling or cutting. Experts should regularly sharpen your drilling and cutting tools in order to make your job simpler.

2. Cleaning after use

Cleaning your tools after every use is an important step in preserving and improving woodwork. Dirt, dirt, and other debris might be the cause of your woodworking tool not cutting or drilling holes like you expect. Before the instruments are put back in their storage areas, wash them thoroughly and dry them.

3. After use, dry the tools

Your tools can be used in rainy, damp environments. Tools should be cleaned before being stored and dried. This reduces the possibility of rust. If this isn't done, you will see your woodwork machinery wear faster than its savage worth.

4. Greasing or oiling

Revolving woodwork tool grease should be applied regularly to eliminate friction that causes wear and tear. It allows your machines to run smoothly and will ensure that you can do woodwork with minimal effort and time. Oiling is also a key component in rust reduction. This prevents woodworking tool corrosive.

5. Reparing or replacing handles

Most woodworking tools are manual. This allows for the handles to wear and tear more quickly. You can get blisters and pain from using a machine without a control handle. This can be avoided by replacing the worn-out handle regularly.

You are a skilled carpenter who wants to do well and get high quality results from your woodworking tools. It is essential to ensure that your woodworking tools are well maintained and properly repaired.

Chapter 7: Basics Of Woodworking

Beginners in woodworking need to know some things. I hope this guide will help them avoid any pitfalls.

Don't worry! Everyone begins somewhere to be a skilled woodworker. Most people don't become master carpenters by the time their first hammer is lifted. While frustration can be frustrating, it's possible to quickly make amazing things with just some practice.

Many newbies fail because they haven't taken the time necessary to understand the fundamentals of creating with wood. They like to challenge someone who has more experience, and they wonder why they are so behind. In these cases you'll often see someone with 30 years experience.

As in many hobbies and career paths, the more you practice skills and spend time learning fundamentals, the better your chances of success. It is possible to acquire all skills if one has patience and is committed.

You'll see results when you put your woodwork skills into action. This will teach you simple skills that will enable you to create successful projects and avoid frustration.

These are the basics that will guide you from the beginning to end of your first wooden project.

1. KNOW YOUR FIREWOOD

Comprehension of wood and building form

Many people just dive in to a woodworking project and start without much knowledge.

Before you start woodwork, it's important to first understand the various wood forms and their characteristics.

It is important to understand how wood works. You may be unable to explain why your boards are splitting or the wood splitting every time you drill.

The study of wood will give you a great advantage in your woodworking skills and help you to avoid mistakes.

Certain woods are better suited to certain ventures than others. Some woods can easily be used and are lightweight, while others can prove to be extremely heavy. Oak, a strong wood, can present unique challenges.

The truth is that wood comes naturally and there are many species of trees. There are many types of wood, including pine, maple oak, cherry poplar and even birch.

Some forests are more suitable than other for different ventures.

For example, if you know that wood shrinks or grows according to temperature and humidity, this information will help you prepare wood. Make sure you have wood indoors before cutting and building.

You can learn more about wood grain and how it is split and cracked if you are familiar with the basics.

Wood is very absorbent, so it's worth looking into the different glues and adhesives available to mix wood. This consistency is important when you plan to paint on wood.

Apart from understanding the basics of wood forms, wood resources, it's also beneficial to learn important information about wood products and wood purchasing in a woodworking workshop.

From standard dimensional hardwood to finished wood products. Be aware of other important factors such as plywood, lumber manufactured under tension, plywood, organized board (OSB), or fibre-board at medium density.

It may seem daunting at first but it is possible to learn all the wood types. You can spend time in your local wood store exploring the different types of wood. Learn how wood works by taking the time to study it.

2. SET UP A DEDICATED WORKSPACE

It is essential to know how you plan on organizing and setting up your work area before you begin designing.

There is no need to dedicate a full garage or shed for woodworking and construction projects. However, it is essential to have somewhere you can store your tools and materials. A lot of woodworking projects will require space, especially if the goal is to create heavy stuff like furniture.

The process of organizing and building a room can save you time and stress.

I don't know how many carpenters are frustrated by their lack of organization. You might know someone like this. They can't remember the exact location of the device they need or have to clear out an overwhelming amount of material from a different project to get to where they are supposed to be.

This dilemma can easily be avoided. Healthy organizational habits can begin early. Don't wait till the "actual shoproom" is ready. Get organized immediately and you'll be able create anything from anywhere. You don't need much space. But you do need a specific place to put it.

This will make it easy to find it and to use it safely.

3. RESPECT YOUR TOOLS AND PRACTICEWOODWORKING SAFETY

You have to respect the tools until you get there.

Safety can seem tedious and unnecessary. But many people don't know better yet end up in the emergency rooms each year due to not using their equipment correctly or neglecting basic safety precautions.

Many injuries can often be prevented.

Learn the Uses of Different Tools

There are many tools to choose form for your projects. However, some tools will be more effective than others for certain tasks. These tools are not all the same.

Also, consider whether you would prefer to use power tools over hand tools. Many woodworkers work with both power tools and hand tools. It is worth understanding the various options to help you choose the right one.

There are many woodworking ideas, and many wonderful tools that can be used to make them. Before purchasing any tool, the first thing you should ask is: What kind or type of stuff are you looking to build?

You can determine which resources will be most effective for your work by understanding what you want. This helps you control your production costs and inventory. There are several tools that you might need, in addition to the simple tools that are necessary for all timber workers.

Cabinet Making Tools*

Furniture Making Tool*

Wood Carving Tools

Knowing about all the types of devices saves time and money. There are only one or two types of saws that you will need.

This brings us up to the next lesson woodworkers must master.

5. START WITH A PROJECT and LEARN TO READ WINDOW WORKING

PLANS

It's much easier to learn if a project has been first created and verified. Woodworking plans can often include a setlist or materials as well as instructions and guidelines for construction.

Woodworking plans may be difficult to understand. Most plans for woodworking include at minimum a list indicating the materials to be used and the size of each piece. This will save you lots of time and stress.

6. UNDERSTANDING THE WOODWORKING PLAN

You have the space, you have the equipment and the safety tips. Now, it's time that you really dive into the process to learn how to build it from beginning to end.

Most woodworking designs have all steps.

Sometimes,

different,

The same from start until finish.

The same steps should be followed every time you make something. Knowing the basics of woodworking will help you save time and frustration when creating your own projects.

Although every woodworker has a unique routine and method of doing things, most follow these steps for the construction of a job:

Select a Project

Gather Supplies* and Materials

Make a Cut Liste

Examine the Build Strategy

Measure the wood and cut it

Assemble The Wood

Apply a Protective Finish on the Wood

Once you've learned the basics of the process, you can start to build a system that will work for your whole project. You are more likely to make errors or get disorganized if all of these things are done simultaneously.

7. MASTERING THE COUT: HOW TO MEASURE & CUT WOOD

AFFORDABLY

Knowing how to correctly calculate is another important skill to have when you first start woodworking. If you don't know how the right way to cut straight and evenly, it can be difficult to get two boards the exact same size.

Not only will it save you time, but you'll also be able to save a lot money if you learn how to properly cut wood. You can save lots of money by buying longer boards you are able to cut yourself.

8. LEARN HOW to ASSEMBLE and JOIN WOOD

The basics of how to correctly combine two pieces are just as important as wood and tools. Your life will be easier if you know how to put the wood pieces together.

It all depends upon the project. You will need to learn many types and brands of adhesives. There are many different ways to combine wood with different finishes.

There are many ways to put it together, which makes the process even more enjoyable. It is essential that you learn dry fitting before you attempt to put anything together. But woodworking clamps are your best friend for almost any situation.

9. PROTECTING YOUR CREATIONS. BEST PRACTICES for SANDING & FISHING WOOD

If your project was completed successfully, you are now ready to move on to the next phase, which is to sand your part and provide security.

Woodworkers need to be able to sand and finish their projects. It ensures that designs are appreciated and succeed for many more decades.

Sanding furniture will provide a smooth surface, even if you opt to cover it with a clear stain or paint. This will make sure no one gets splintered in the process of using your product. There are many methods of sanding wood.

Next, apply a protective coat to the piece once it has been sanded. The type and use of the item, as well as the projects you've worked on, will impact the type of protective coating you use.

Chapter 8: How To Grow Your Business Using The Chain Markets

Once the products are made, where do they go? A pattern of selling is the most important thing for any woodworking business. It may begin small, selling to friends and neighbors. You will eventually see it grow and sell them on your own website.

Community Selling

Community selling is when items are sold within social networks and in the local community. These websites include Etsy, Craigslist, eBay, and Craigslist. Each one has its advantages and disadvantages, so let's review each.

eBay-This is an online shopping site that's like a bazaar with many products. It's often what people first think of when they want to purchase a particular product at a very cheap price. This website's pro is that it has billions upon billions of visitors every day. The downside is that there is a lot to choose from and you can lose out on a lot of potential customers.

Craigslist: This website is local and allows you to buy products within a 50-mile radius. This is a great option if your goal is to keep order quantities small and to offer customers a customized option. You'll find that, even as you climb up the market chain, you will still advertise to this website throughout the process, just like other businesses. This website comes with a con. You don't have much protection, and there are many people who have experienced horror stories through this website. You will often need to earn the trust and respect of any person you do business. There is usually a low profit range on almost all products, so it is unlikely that you can charge a price you consider appropriate.

Etsy is a site for artists and crafts people who sell their work as a hobby. This makes it the con to your business. It will allow you to deal with a lot of competition from other individuals offering the same work you do. Etsy has a lot of people who are very particular about their projects. It is not possible to just make a model and sell it. Although you could make this work at the local level of selling, you'll find that it requires more carpentry skill to make high-income from this site.

Local Business Listing

The next step of the process is to market your product to local business. This can prove to be challenging and even difficult. You need to begin going into local businesses and finding out if you are able make a product for them. Target and

Walmart will most likely reject your product as you are unable to mass produce it. However, small shops that specialize in unique furniture will be open to your offer if the quality of your goods is good. This is where you'll need to grow your business in terms of staff and have an adequate insurance policy in place in case something that you make causes injury to a client.

These types of businesses are looking for a way to sell a product. If you are selling local products, it is likely that you delivered the product pre-built to your customers. Most products sold to local business are packaged in smaller parts. Because it saves space, the shop may want to keep several items in stock so that customers can request them.

Your product will be most easily sold by any business that sells at a Farmer's Market. It is a local gathering of people selling their own goods. Products that are mass-produced can be taken on by any type of furniture rental business. Tent Rental companies often ordered large quantities of furniture. This was a common problem I saw when I worked there. Because of their unique design and quality, they often ordered local woodworkers. A brown wooden stool that had been polished and cost 30 dollars to make would often be sold at 100 dollars per piece. However, it was rented for only two to five cents per piece.

Warehouse Selling

Warehouse selling is for people who are skilled in mass producing woodworking products. Lowes', Walmart's, Target, and Home Depot all fall under this category. They prefer brands with a good reputation that produce quality work. The return window for selling the product is short. This is because it requires you to meet with the owner of the entire district, or an individual who has control over large numbers of businesses in the area. Anyone lower than that will most likely reject your proposal to sell your product in their stores.

It is restricted to those who can mass-produce a product because many of the people who shop there for these types are D.I.Y. Individuals who can't afford to buy pre-made products or are unwilling to buy them. An example of such a customer would be one who buys a cheap cabinet. The cabinet typically consists of five panel cut panels, two panels with a plastic handle and a couple screws. You can use twenty dollars to create a plan that uses every piece wood in a single large-panel panel. Next, you will need to purchase the parts, paint and polish. You could spend ten minutes making each piece of wood, and another ten minutes painting them all.

This is the part where mass production is a necessity. Normally, the paint must dry for at least a day. This is a loss of valuable time. With a hundred bucks, you could make more cabinets, but still fall within the same category as waiting time. Lowes or Walmart would want to order as many products as possible on their demand.

If you don't have the time or money to wait, then you need an automated method that uses machines to complete most of the work. That is why most woodworkers stay away from this market. While you may be able sell more high-quality products if they are well-made, the chances of making low volumes of them are slim. The reason for this is that woodworkers rarely make such products due to the possibility of replacing many of their items with metal products. This market is not easy to enter but can yield a large profit. A bed frame would be an example of such high profit margins. This usually sells at least two hundred dollars. A king size bed frame has three boards on the headboard that support the mattress. It also includes two boards from the front that move from the side to the back.

This frame could be made in a matter of hours and cost around one to two hundred bucks. It is possible to sell a similar frame for as much as it took to produce it, but it will cost you thousands of dollars depending upon the design and quality.

Web Selling

Web Selling is another type of selling. This type allows you to choose the type and quantity of work you wish to produce. Singular selling means that you have created a blueprint for a specific type and price of custom work. This works like this:

A customer will go to the site and find a product they like.

The buyer will choose to get a quotation on the product. This is the best option for you to fit your woodworking products into your schedule. Additionally, you can mass manufacture products that are quick to put together and have a limit for how much you can order. This helps to stop any rental company or consumer ordering more than you can make. This market offers opportunities to do more than simply woodwork. This stage can help you sell courses, market your brand on your website and even offer tutoring to those who are financially able. This stage of the sale process makes the most money, but also allows for the most flexibility and product choice.

The problem with your website is that you will need a lot of people to manage it. This is the best way to keep your website simple. If you are going to make any money online, it will need to be targeted at people who want your product.

Companies that sell woodworking products online usually have their own automated process. They have also negotiated a deal for a manufacturing partner, have enough employees, or have simply placed all products on a quote basis. It's either that you have enough people who can provide product fast or that you plan everything to avoid becoming overwhelmed by orders.

Chapter 9: Coffee Mug Rack

This coffee cup rack project is sure for a fan of hot coffee, tea, or chocolate. It doesn't take too long depending on the level of your skills and the tools available. As long as your children are involved in the process, you can supervise them and assist with the heavier steps.

To build a cupholder, you don't necessarily need to follow these directions. You can modify the spacing of the hooks to create a potholder or a place where you can store a variety of kitchen items. This could be a good option for people who lack space but want an attractive and affordable solution.

You may need to clean up your pallet with the power washer before you get started. You'll likely hang your drinking glasses on it and keep it somewhere you store and prepare food.

What you'll require

One pallet

Wood screws

Hooks for holding your mugs

Paint and stencil are available for creating a sign on your rack if you choose.

Sandpaper

Tape measure

Right angle ruler

Pencil

Circular saw

Safety goggles

Cordless drill

Screwdriver

Making This Project

Unless you have an extremely small pallet, it's unlikely that you will need the entire thing. You can pick the section that looks the best and add the middle joint to stabilize it.

Use the pencil for marking the spot you want to use the right angle ruler. The area you mark will determine the size of your rack.

You can also use a circular saw to trim your pallet. However, a hand saw works better but at a slower clip. This will result in a miniature pallet and a strong structure.

Sand the wood where you are cutting it. Make sure the wood is smooth and free from sharp edges and splinters.

You can paint something such as "COFFEE" or "MUGS" at the top of the picture, as shown in this image. Use a stencil. Or, you can draw it yourself with a pen and paper.

You are allowed to create this rustically, since that is the whole idea behind pallets. You can use a ruler, tape measure or ruler to mark the spots you want to place your hooks. You can make it even. However, you might want some creativity with your placements. Because of the handmade nature of this rack, it doesn't matter if your work isn't perfect.

Make the holes that will hold the screws. But, make sure the drill bit is smaller than the actual screws.

Use your screws to attach the cups' hooks.

Your drinks mug rack now is complete!

Deck Chair

This next project can be very helpful for anyone who wants friends over to grill or just to enjoy a good time around a great fire but doesn't have somewhere to sit.

You don't want to take your indoor chair outside and risk getting it dirty or wet.

These "Adirondack-style" chairs are ideal for building with pallet timber. People often assume that useful furniture has to be complicated and expensive to create. It isn't true.

Keep in mind, these chairs will be exposed and subject to all kinds of weather. They will likely be outside most of their lives. Weather-resistant screws, glews, paint and other things that can be damaged by rain, wind or snow are good options.

What you will require

If you have a large collection of chairs, one should suffice.

Screws (for outdoor use)

Wood glue (waterproof).

Jig saw

Compound miter saw

Power drill

Driver

Table saw

Belt sander

Palm sander

Safety goggles

These items can sometimes be replaced by hand-powered tools. Be ready to put in some hard work.

Making This Project

You'll have to cut planks out of your pallet. Every pallet will be unique in shape and size so you need to use your judgment. To see how the frame is assembled, take a look at this picture.

Once you are satisfied with the dimensions of your pieces and the chairs you will be using, glue and then attach the basic frame. It is possible to use clamps to secure the frame until the glue dries. Otherwise, you can use the screws.

Take two pieces from wood and make the accross section of your seat. Next, lay plank pieces on your back to create a comfortable flat portion. Can you see the rounded top of this seat back? You can modify this to create the desired effect.

Place planks over the frame to make the seat.

Now you can attach the seat back on to the frame.

Sand everything down, then paint or finish the wood however you prefer.

Shipping Crate Storage Box

Ok, so this next project doesn't actually involve a pallet build. You can use packing crates to make pallets, but people all over the planet have been getting into upcycling. If you are able to find packing crates, then why not make something from them? The best thing about this table? You can open the top and keep the contents inside.

The best part of using packing crates as a building material is that the basic shapes are already available. Just get creative and finish the job.

What you'll want

You have the option of using 4 blocks as legs, or wheels if your preference is for a mobile table.

2 Hinges

Use the handle on your lid

Use a plywood sheet as the lid.

Power drill, screwdriver

Screws

Sandpaper

Paint or finisher? It's your choice, but a paint-resistant finisher may be useful to keep spills off the table.

Making This Project

Before you start, you should sand down the entire crate. Be careful not to leave any sharp edges, or splinters on the crate that could cause injury.

This is also an excellent time to finish your container or weatherproof it, if you'd like.

Attach the wooden legs or wheels using your drill and screwdriver to the bottom. For extra strength, place these around the corners of the container.

Attach your hinges to your plywood at the corners.

Chapter 10: Stationary Tools

The first thing that pops into your mind when you think about woodworking is portable, hand-held instruments. You should not overlook the importance of stationary machines for woodworking. Mobile tools are absolutely necessary for connecting, assembling and general "putting together" a woodpiece. However, stationary machines can play an integral role in shaping woodpieces prior to construction.

Mobile tools may be used to put the blocks together. However, stationary tools must be used as the block builders. Stationary woodworking instruments shape the woodpieces for the final assembly.

These are the most frequently found stationary machines in woodshops.

The Workbench

The focal point of all woodworking activities should be your workbench. Most workbenches are available in small trays that can be hidden beneath the bench. This will allow you to keep your smaller tools organized and minimize clutter in the woodshop.

It doesn't really matter if your bench is bought or built. The bench will be subjected to high levels of stress, so it needs to be sturdy and reliable. It should also be equipped with a place to attach vices, clamps, and other hardware. You must keep your workbench clean, and it should be in a well-lit place.

Bench Grinder

Bench grinders are essentially an abrasive sanding wheel. It's simple to imagine how a Bench Grinder operates. As with most stationary tools and machines, the bench grinder needs to be "fed" the wooden piece. The operator must learn to operate the woodpiece, and not just the tool.

These bench grinders can be used for buffing or polishing as well as sanding. For example, a woodworker would use a bench grinder to polish a cabinet door.

The tool can be used with various materials depending on the type of wheels and the quality of the wheel attached. The purchase of a bench grinder will often include a package with wheels. The quality of the wheel will determine the project the tool can accomplish.

Buffering, also known as fine grade, grinding wheels, allow bench grinders the ability to polish all types of materials, such as metal, wooden, and plastic. High-grade wheels are used for reforming rough metal before fitting or welding. These wheels have a high quality finish that will allow the bench grinder sharpen your tools. It is important to inspect all cutting tools such as drill bits, saw blades and mortisers for dullness.

Securely mount your bench grinder on a stable support structure such a pillar, bench, or table. Make sure that your tool comes with an emergency shutoff.

Jointers

Many woodworkers use jointers to make wood joints as accurately and quickly as possible. Joints are necessary for making biscuit join and mortise arrangements. A jointer makes it easy to fix them. More than this, a jointer guarantees a precise joint cut, minimising mistakes and saving the woodworker valuable time.

Drill Press

The drill press is similar to the bench grinder in that it can perform multiple tasks. Drill presses can be equipped with drilling bits to make boring holes. They also come with grinding wheels, which can be used to polish or grind.

However, the assembly of the drill presses is more complex than that for a bench grinder. It consists of a pillar, column, table, base, a drillhead, and a spindle. The drillhead follows a predetermined path through the column. The drill heads is placed on the table of the press, and the drill descends to the wood. This creates greater accuracy when drilling.

The drill press, which is more fixed than portable, is typically available in a mounted format. This requires that it be secured to a stable surface (e.g. a workbench) or to the floor. The drill press, also called the bench drill, pedestal drill or pillar or pillar drill is comprised primarily of a tablet, table, spindle or drill head, spindle, drill heads, and column or pillar.

Induction motors power the drill press. Three handles are located on the drillhead that enable the user to operate the power tools. These handles can be found on the core hub and are used to control the drill vertically.

The drill press table is adjustable vertically to adjust for the size of the woodpiece being cut.

Drill presses have many advantages over hand drills. Drill presses have the advantage of being more precise and secure, as they require a clamp to place the woodpiece. This prevents it from sliding. Drill presses also make it quicker and easier to bore multiple holes through a woodpiece.

Band Saw

The bandsaw is a motor-powered, motor-powered saw. A narrow band of toothed metallic constitutes the "cutting elements" and is often used in lumbermills.

Band saws come in miniature versions. They are hand-held power tools, and can only be used in fixed positions. Bands of toothed, revolving blades are powered by a motor and ride on two wheels in a horizontal plane. Most band saws are able to adjust their wheels. The space between the wheels determines the type of cuts the band saw will make.

The tool can make curved cuts by adjusting the width of the blade. This makes band saws great for cutting irregularly shaped shapes.

For timber mills, band saws are more preferred to circular saws because there is less waste. Band saws can be used to cut smaller sizes, or kerfs, which helps minimize wastage.

Band saw blades come in a range of sizes: 4 inches wide x 19 feet long x 22 GA thickness, up to 16 feet wide X 62 feet long x 11 GA thickness. A timber yard generally chooses a bigger blade. They are often stretched very tight considering the size and shape of the wood they are making.

There are many types and sizes of large bandsaws.

Resaws are a common type of larger-sized band saw and most likely to found in a timbermill. They are precise, fast, and have small kerf sizes.

Double cut saws have cutting teeth that are on both sides of their blades, just like the name. The size of a double-cut saw is similar to that of a traditional head saw. However, this saw can cut "backwards" in a similar way.

Head saws are used mainly to make first cuts in logs. A rotating tooth on a headsaw's blade is made up of two to three inches of space between the saw and its sharp edge. These teeth can also have silver teeth that are located at the back of it's sharp edge. This is an extremely useful feature for when a bandsaw must back out of a cut.

Band saws are great for general cutting, but they can't be used for more precise work. Instead, think of band saws as the initial step in your woodworking project. These are great for making pieces that can be reworked later.

Wood Lathe

The wood lathe can be used to spin wood for various tasks including deformation, drilling or sanding. It is very similar in appearance to a pottery wheel. In which clay is placed at the spinning mount point, it can be shaped.

Woodworkers can make woodpieces with the help of a woodlathe. The wood lathe is a specialized tool used to create different shapes from blocks of wood. Popular examples of wood lathe-related products include table legs (chair legs), cue sticks (cue sticks) and baseball bats.

Most wood lathes are similar. The wood is attached the the lathe's top stock, also known as leg stock or the spindle. A horizontal rail sits between the operator's head stock and the headstock, acting as a rest. The head stock spins wooden pieces. The operator may then use shaping instruments, most often hand-held.

Another wood lathe specialty is the rotary one. It can be used for peeling bark off softwood logs. Adjusted calibration allows sharp blades successfully to be positioned to peel continuous or semicontinuous rolls from unwanted parts of the log.

Specialized wood turning machines allow operators to create unique shapes beyond the traditional cylindrical design. They can also make wooden bowls or pots. While the wood lathes may be very different in appearance, the basic operating principles will remain the same.

Craft workers have a lot of options: the watchman's lute, glasswork lathe, ornamental tuning lap lathe, and metal lute make their lives easier. They all use the same basic principles and serve a similar purpose to wood lathes. The wood lathes can be used to quickly and easily shape woodpieces.

Chapter 11: The Woodworking Router (And Its Supporting Tool)

The Woodworking Router, a popular tool in the hardwood industry, is an indispensable tool. These machines are well-liked by pattern makers and designers of stairways because of their simplicity and ability to create complex and basic wood patterns. Because of its versatility, the machinery is becoming more popular in the cabinet industry.

Before the advent of power tools, the hand-tools of this type consisted of a large hand plane made from wood and a narrow knife that protruded across the base plate. This design was nicknamed "Old Woman's Tooth" for its similarity of form. Its multiple benefits allowed woodworkers to develop new products.

Despite the advent of newer powertools, the first-hand tool is still highly sought after by carpenters and woodworkers. Electric routers were invented because of the increased development required. This improvement led to the development today's many router parts. This is a quick overview of today's most advanced tool.

Types Of Routers

Woodworking routers come in two types: the mounted or handheld. The type of tool you use will dictate the size of your project. The table-mounted equipment requires a supporting worktable. This unit is ideal for creating delicate, smaller pieces. Turning router bits upside down allows for more precise cutting. These units are safer because wood parts can be secured and secured. It is the ideal choice for those who are just starting out in woodwork or want to become a professional.

These handheld units usually have large handles, with the motor located in the Centre on each side. This is to make it easier to move the parts. It allows the user to have maximum control over the machine. Some features may not be available in new models. A dust collection system which vacuums the sawdust is a popular option. It's particularly impressive if there isn't a suitable workshop for your projects.

There are many options for bits and pieces to fit your router. Every type of diameter can have different effects upon wood or any other material. Professionals and hobbyists love half-inch bits.

These parts are stiffer and produce better cuts. These bits have less vibration. It is less fragile and easier to handle, which allows you create beautiful designs.

Some online retailers sell custom router bits, which can be tailored to meet your cutting needs. These bits are handy for delicate projects like restoration and smaller materials. These tools are great if your project involves the application of original moldings and woodwork trims.

Buy your router and bits. Before you examine your options, you should consider what you will use the router to create or repair. Get advice from carpenters and builders as well as staff at hardware companies to help you find the best solution. There are potential dangers when using a woodworking routing machine. You need to have adequate protection equipment, such as safety glasses, gloves and pillows. These items will help ensure your safety during the construction process.

Woodworking routers and router bit-the right tools today's homeowners

Is it possible to make a piece from wood? Let's see you helping to repair wooden items. Did you think of using machines to aid you with future tasks? If yes to all of these questions, you might consider buying woodworking routers & bits.

A Working Router for Woodworking

It is a powertool that can be used to create many shapes and forms in wood. This machine is frequently used to make structures on the edges of wooden panels.

The tool that we see today is nothing but a fragment of its history. The router was an ordinary hand tool that consisted of a large, simple wooden plane and a blade with a small diameter. This was before electric-operated machines were made. The woodworkers and capitals gave this unusual appearance its "Old Woman's Tooth".

These routers were used to create staircase designs and patterns by patternmakers. They can make complex designs from simple shapes. These devices proved very useful to the cabinet industry. The cabinets and cupboards were designed with care and attracted many customers who bought them.

Even though electric equipment was on the market, the manual device was still in high demand. Many workers and producers praised its utility and continued using it until more was produced. This led to the development of electric tools in the United States, and other industrialized countries.

There are many types

There are two types available today: Table and hand-held routers. Handheld buttons can be placed either on the motor body or one side of the handle. This device typically has two handles per side and a central motor. This feature makes it easier to control the machine. It can be used to cut or shape wood and glide smooth.

Table routers are machines that can be attached to a table. They are great for smaller pieces that need more design details. This is why both professionals and amateur woodworkers often refer to their utility. It is also useful for novices, provided that the wood is properly secured.

The Bits of the Router

Router bits is a tool that's used to make routers. These bits are available in many sizes, and each one has a specific function. For example, straight bits can be used to make vertical or straight cuts. It can also be used for hollowing out wood. If an employee is attached to a special router, they can show their efficiency by showing how much material they have removed in increments.

These instruments are worth having

DIY wood projects can be completed by buying. With the right materials, practice, and the right tools, you can also fix and restore wooden furniture.

It is simple to purchase woodworking routers or bits online. Look for reviews from customers and business owners that are available online at affordable prices.

How to Purchase Woodworking Routers and Bits

While woodworking may seem difficult, it is also rewarding. With the right experience and time you can manage small projects with repairs. Here are some tips and tricks about routers.

Woodwork router can be used for design, manufacturing, and repair of wood furniture. Its capabilities allow users create layouts and cut existing patterns. It was used for as many years as wood was used over hundreds of years.

The woodworking router used be operated manually. Today, it is powered electrically. There are many options for combo and fixed-base woodworking router kits.

The engine of a plunge router is attached at the base by a spring. This router type is the most safest, since it can be held above the wood. Its ability plunge allows for precise and safe results. Many versions feature 1.75 horsepower and 100 Vs functionality.

Fixed-base engines can range from 1.75 to 3 horsepower. They can also be adjusted by raising or decreasing the engine at their base. This is the most easily accessible type for students.

Wood can be easily cut by enthusiasts or carpenters working together. The machine can be adjusted to make cuts as small as 0.1 millimeters.

Also known as laminate routers or trim routers (or smaller), trim routers can be used for cutting. The machine's set horsepower is approximately one hp. This machine was instantly popular because it is simpler to use. The machine is small and easy-to-use. Users can operate it without any training. This tool is ideal for laminating surfaces, as it can make precise cuts.

Combination woodworking tools include a medium-sized, fixed-base and plunge base engine. Combining both fixed and plunge routers, it is like having two tools. It can work with handheld and table-mounted routers.

Router bits, or router pieces, are attachments for woodworking machines. Each bit can be used for a variety of purposes and comes in different sizes. Straight bits, such as vertical and horizontal cutters, are available in a variety of sizes. These router bits also work well when solid wood is hollowed-out or shaped.

Attachments for flush cutting will require cutting bits. These instruments are equipped with a pilot of the exact same size as their cutting radius. When used in patterns, the bearing serves as a useful guide and can create multiple identical shapes.

Chapter 12: How To Create Bracket Feet

Ogee bracket feet which are often associated with the Chippendale style were in use since the end of the seventeenth century and remain among the most recognizable styles in furniture. The distinctive S-curve on the faces as well as the intricate profiles at the sides of the feet were traditionally constructed using hand-tools, which is a long-lasting labour-intensive procedure. My approach blends the best features of old and new. I've replaced the molding planes using the tablesaw to smooth out the ogee shape, and the bandsaw is replacing the coping saw to cut the final profile. However, machines cannot replace scrapers or other tools that are necessary for reworking the shapes cut by machines.

Begin with table sawing

* The front pair of feet usually have mitered.
* To ensure the most perfect flow and grain match and to maximize efficiency, start with a large blank milled to the correct size.
* You'll need a piece of wood that is long enough to create six pieces.
* You'll also need materials to construct the un-fashioned parts of the rear pair of feet, that are put dovetailed to each other. The majority of these pieces were constructed of secondary wood since they were not visible.
* The most important thing to do is to create a few full-size patterns from 1/8-inch thick plywood. This will help guide the machine and handwork.

* I use an example pattern for drawing an Ogee profile on the opposite side of my blank.

* Once the ogee shape is completed I use a different pattern to draw the miters as well as trace the outline on the inside part of my foot.

* To speed up and ensure stability, I form the entire face of the blank on the tablesaw using a technique of cove-cutting.

* This is accomplished by transferring the piece in a diagonal fashion across the blade supported by an auxiliary fence, then raising the blade slightly with each passing.

* You can use any straight material to make the fence, so long as it's strong enough to hold the workpiece.

* The fencing I designed is made up of two 3/4-inch thick pieces of MDF.

After connecting the pieces I tore both long edges in straight.

* I don't have any special blades for the cove cut. It's just a blade combination. This cove cut is an asymmetrical cut that means the blade is parallel to the table. An cove that is not symmetrical would require that the blade be tilted.

Start by raising the blade until the edge of the cove applying the pattern as a guide.

* You can now dial in the length of the cove, by pivoting the fence auxiliary.
* Put the top of the pattern on the fence.
* To ensure precision ensure accuracy, use the top of a combination square in order to keep the pattern in a 90-degree angle towards the table and fence.

If your eyes are level to the table, rotate the fence until it is aligned with the cutout on the pattern.

* Secure the fence to create the test cut.
* To do this reduce the blade until it's 1/16 inch higher than the table.
* Perform the first pass or two, and then check your cut to the pattern you traced

on the bottom on the sheet.

* Since you're making such gentle cuts, any errors in the installation can be fixed by changing the fence in the course of your work.

* Continue to make passes across the blade, lifting the blade about 1/16 inch at a stretch, until you've cut the entire length of your cove.

After the cove has been cut off, it's now time to design the convex part of the foot blank.

This task is started on the tablesaw, with the blank on the edge.

* Rotate the blade to get rid of the majority from the debris in a single pass.

* Adjust the blade angle until it is creeping higher along the layout line by using smaller passes.

* You'll get a the appearance of a faceted surface.

How do you form the convex portion
* After following the layout lines at the bottom of the piece, smooth out the marks of the machine on the blank, and then refine the curves.
* To form the convex area I use No. 5 Jack and No. 4 smoother planes, slowly taking away the tablesawn facets in order to create smooth curve.
* To smooth the concave surface I use an sandpaper scraper and gooseneck scraper.
* Finally, I sand the curves to smooth. After the face is completed then you can begin cutting individual feet from the blank, and then mitering them.
* In keeping with the periods, I typically cut the front pair of feet, but I use half-blind dovetails for the rear pair.
* Dovetails are a sturdy method of joining the flat, thin back piece to the fashioned. To ensure a consistent fit of the grains between those feet in front it is essential to arrange the parts in pairs. After laying

out the pieces make sure you leave some additional material on the straight-cut ends.

* This will allow you enough room to make trial cuts until you've got the perfect miters.

Once the miters are cut, trim all feet to their length using the inside profile design as a reference.

Dovetails should be cut in the feet's rear pair Tails on the flat feet , and sockets on the feet that are molded.

* Don't put any of the feet at this point.

How to determine the foot's profile

* When the joining is complete, lay the feet down and then cut out the inner profile of the feet.

* Copy the full-size design for drawing the pattern and bandsaw the design close to lines.

The feet should be glued to the miters as

well as the dovetails.

* For miters, I use clamping cauls, which redirect the clamping force onto the curves. I also ensure that I seal or size the grain's porous ends using glue prior to assembling.
* The glue needs to be completely dry to effectively finish the grain else, joint could be damaged.

It might seem odd to apply glue to the feet before fairing the profile at the end however, it does make it much easier to hold the feet into a vise prior to the final shape.

* Once the glue has dried clean the inside contour.

First, I get rid of all bandsaw marks by using file and rasps.

* I then use gouges and chisels to cut the shapes at an angle.
* The back cut helps to refine only the visible portion of the profile on the front using files and rasps.

* I also break the edges of the outside by chamfering them using the chisel.

The last step is to install strengthening corner blocks to the outside of feet.

The blocks reinforce the miter, and also add to the overall glue exterior fixing the feet to the base frame.

Here's a way to avoid a problem using cross-grain glue on the vertical part.

*I cut out a number of glue blocks in small pieces and stacked them, changing their grain directions.

* This makes a very robust block assembly that will remain indefinitely.

* There's no requirement to secure one of the blocks of glue in the first place. A simple rub joint can accomplish the job.

* When the glue is dry in the block, I cut the vertical pieces to be flush and then chisel a small chamfer around the corner to ensure that the pieces cannot be observed by prying eyes.

Chapter 13: How To Construct Drafters

If it's a tiny drawer in a jewelry case or the large, deep drawer of a dresser each drawer is nothing more than a container that can slide through an opening. There are a myriad of combinations of building methods which can be utilized to create this box. If you know the different ways of making drawers it will be possible to choose the most suitable building method to build your dream that will give you the perfect combination of strength, beauty and performance. Drawers can be constructed of hardwood, plywood or both. The fronts of drawers are often the main focal point of an object, displaying a stunning figures of molded edges, elegant pulls. The front of the drawer can be integrated into the drawer, which means that it is directly joined to the sides of the drawer, or connected to a built drawer box. The options for joining at the front and back be as simple as butt joints to traditional hand-cut dovetails. The bottom of drawers can be made out of plywood or solid wood. To properly size a drawer it is important to understand not only the dimension of the opening but also how deep the inside. Drawers may be designed to be flush to or recessed into or even overlapping over the top of the casing. Different types of furniture demand various kinds of drawers. A drawer constructed of plywood with a fake front would make sense for a shop cabinet however, it is unsuited to an 18th century reproduction in high-end style. The materials and joinery you choose must match the kind of furniture you're planning to construct. The same goes for the way the drawer is able to slide into and out of its pockets. Let's start there.

High-level overview

As with all drawer choices The options for sliding drawers vary from simple and effective to exquisitely handmade.

The sides of a drawer made of wood are able to slide directly onto the wooden frame inside the case.

The majority of drawers with integrated fronts work well when paired with this design since the drawer's dimensions are built to be able to accommodate the opening.

* Made-to-order drawer slides are popular in kitchen cabinets, but they're becoming used in increasing numbers on luxury furniture in the present.

Although they're snubbed by some purists slide designs can be fitted quickly and effortlessly and are difficult to fault their soft-close mechanisms and the ability to extend fully.

* They can be mounted on either the bottom or side and are great to use with false-front drawers, or drawers that have sliding dovetails.

* Every type of commercial slide comes with specific requirements for drawers So you'll need create the drawer in order to hold the slides.

For example, side-mounted slides generally require 1/2 inch area on the sides and bottom of the box.

* If you're using slide slides from a commercial company, it's an excellent idea to keep them in your possession before you begin building either the case or drawers.

No matter if it has an integral front , or an untrue front, the majority of strains from pulling and racking in a drawer box happen in the front curves. since the drawer is open and shut by pushing and pulling on the front.

* Any movement that isn't straight into or

out of the drawer pocket can cause strain on the racking mechanism, which hits the front-corner joints the most.

* To this end front-corner joints must be as sturdy as is possible and include a specific mechanical reinforcement.

* This connection could be as simple as pins or pegs in the rabbet joint or it could be the interlocking power of the half-blind dovetail as it is known today.

It's also essential to have a sturdy mechanical joint in the bottom of your drawer the aesthetics of the drawer are less of a concern since the curves aren't often noticed.

* Because of this, rear-corner joints can be distinct from front-corner joint.

* If you're using the machine to cut the front joinery it is logical to utilize the same setups for cutting the joinery on back.

Bottoms of drawers

* The materials you select and the style of the drawer's bottom is dependent on the design of drawer you're building and whether you want a simple shop drawer or one designed for a secretary from the 18th century.
* Both plywood and solid wood are often used to make drawer bottoms.
Wood is the standard choiceand, visually it's hard to beat.
But you have to permit solid lumber to contract and expand in response to changes in humidity to ensure that it does not cause the drawer to be bounded within its opening.
The Plywood option is more durable option for drawer bottoms because it doesn't expand and contract as the changes in humidity as solid wood.
* Although reproduction builders and a

handful of traditionalists aren't keen on tops made of plywood, it's simple to claim their superiority.

* A bottom of plywood could be completely housed by grooves on both the back and front, and then glued in place to reinforce your drawer.

* It could be pulled through the back and then screwed onto the back of the drawer or fixed and glued on the top of a drawer with a fake front

Chapter 14: The Use Of Specialized Metal Fasteners

The majority of joints in wood depend on fasteners made of metal. While some joints may require glue and some are formed using interlocking components like nails, screws bolts, as well as a range of special steel connectors offer woodworkers the most rapid, efficient methods of joining. Many of these fasteners are on the market, either conventional or specialized, that it is difficult to choose the right one for a particular task difficult. The choice must consider the strength needed to join the piece, as well as the likelihood that the joint might require dismantling in the future , as well as the significance of the appearance. The most conventional approach to the majority of issues in joining finished or rough pieces of wood, consult The Best Fastener for Every Job to help you choose the right fasteners to complete the job.

Nails, one of the most commonly used fasteners, are simple and simple to use. They're also cheap. As with all metal fasteners they function by friction. the force of a driven nail is displaces wood fibers, and they clamp the shank to keep it in the desired position. But nails with large, sharp points even though they can easily penetrate wood and easily, can cause the fibers to split in two. The nails that are blunt, whether they're made in a factory or crafted by hand are more durable since the point that is blunt clears an opening in the wood and creates an unsplit sleeve fibers that wrap around the shank.

When a nail is in position there are two

types of force that can be used to dislodge it. The first of stress, shearing is applied in a direction perpendicular to the shank. The other type, called withdrawal stress is applied parallel from the direction in which the entrance is made. A nail is more resilient to shearing than stress for withdrawal, and should be driven along the grain so that the primary force applied to it, after it has been put there, is shearing force.

Screws are more durable than nails against tension due to their threads having an increased surface area, which results in more friction with wood fibers. Additionally, they are simple to remove without damaging or tearing wood. They're more expensive than nails, and require more time to set up. Before you can join the two wood pieces together you need to make at least one pilot hole.

Nuts and bolts aren't as frequently used than nails and screws because both bolt ends have to be easily accessible, which is which is not possible in all situations. However, they can create extremely strong, tight connections between two pieces that are too big for conventional fasteners. Some fasteners are specific. For finishing work, splines are metal plates that are thin, and toothed or corrugated fasteners create tight joints in which screws or nails could cut wood, for instance, in counter tops and frames for windows. For rough-built constructions, shaped plates of metal known as anchors or framing connectors are used to secure structural components. The use of glues, although more prevalent in cabinetmaking than home carpentry, increase the durability that any fastener made of metal. The epoxy resins, the casein glue vegetable glue , and synthetic resin glue are all used to join wood.

Types of Nails:

Sizes of the "penny" classification system: Sizes may be confusing because they are based on prices per pound of the past of England. The smallest nail of this rating system is the 2 penny that equals 1 inch, and the largest 60-penny equivalents six inches. A nail longer than 20-penny is generally measured in inches. A nail smaller than two cents is typically measured by fractions of an inch. A lot of nails sold today are priced in inches.

Common nail: smooth shaft, flat head

Box nail: Nearly identical to the common nail, but with a shorter shafts, and is recommended when splitting poses a risk. (Common and box are used for when the appearance of the surface is not important and both are available with a an exterior coating of resin.)

Cut nails Join wood to the masonry or for a rustic look in flooring.

Spiral nails are concealed from view, they securely grip the floor and joists beneath. Duplex nails have two heads. for use for a short period, with the top head is easy to grasp to take off.

Finishing nails and Casing nails Similar to smaller heads. The only difference is that casing has a an additional head to give it a better grip, and both are simple to drive through the surface using the help of a nail set.

Wire brads or wire nails Wire brad or wire nail: the smallest size nails, in fractions of inches for wood with thin thickness.

Screw Types used in Woodworking:
Each has sharp threads with a sharp edges. The sizes the head shape, as well as slotting. Length in inches. diameter measured in measurements in gauges or even fractions. The standard diameters range from No.4 (1/8 millimeter) up to

No.14 (1/4 inches). Certain models do not come with the standard smooth shank. Lag bolts or lag screwsare the biggest screws employed for heavy-duty work. Their hexagonal or square heads can be turned with wrenches. Some have slots that allow them to be turned by screwdrivers too. They are also They are sized in inches to accommodate both the length and the diameter.

Wood screws of standard size: Come with smooth shanks and slotted head They are available in three head types and two slot styles.

Flat-heads are most commonly used because they are simple to countersink under the surface of

Wood surface, and then cover it with putty.

Oval-heads and round-heads are often covered to give a decorative look.

One slot, and Phillips slots are both equally popular You will require a separate screwdriver designed for Phillips however, you'll can control screws head.

Standard screws are measured by the diameter of gauge numbers as well as with lengths in inches

Standard gauges include No.4 (1/8 millimeter diameter) up to No.14 (1/4-inch diameter).

Sheet metal screws are made of threads that extend beyond the heads and are employed in woodworking, specifically for the purpose of attaching plywood panels as well as hardware. They are available in three standard head shapes as well as the fourth, which is known as pan heads, and includes either standard or Phillips slots. They're sized similarly to typical wood screws.

Bolts: Though most often used in metalwork the use of bolts, washers, and nuts are also used for woodwork. Bolts are measured by how large the thread diameter as well as in length, from the top of the head until the point at which the bolt ends. Flat head stove bolts however measure from above the head.

Rail bolts: the best-known connect both rails in a staircase to posts for newel and goosenecks.

Stove bolts: Used to join 2-by-4s in order to create rough shelving machines and carriage bolts that are stronger and heavier, are utilized in headers reinforced with steel.

Finishing Fasteners:

Special fasteners that have sharp edges or teeth that project strengthen weak nail joints between butted parts like counter tops, or the mitered corners on window-screen frames. Splines are less thick than other fasteners and are less noticeable and less noticeable, are employed on heavy pieces in which screws or nails are unattractive and unsafe generally, to connect the two sections of an stair railing, ending to end.

Anchors:
Framing anchors come with a variety of designs, and are designed to accommodate various connections. They were first created in the 1940s to reinforce connections of buildings in areas of hurricanes These anchors are now becoming more popular because they can eliminate toenailing and difficult angle hammering. An anchor is secured to the wood with common nails of eight cents or by smaller nails that are bundled with the anchors by the maker.

Chapter 15: Safety Precautions For Woodworking

A healthy and vital aspect is crucial to any company's wellbeing, both social and economic that's why it is essential to stay clear of occupational hazards to safeguard employees. It is evident that each job is a type of risk or risk but wood workers are exposed to a variety of hazards that the majority of workers are not aware of at work and can increase their risk of advancement.

Here's an overview of the most important safety practices for woodworkers and common woodworking traps and methods to stay clear of them:

4.1 VITAL SAFETY TECHNIQUES

Woodworking is among the most enjoyable activities and the safest you can engage in, provided that you follow an elementary set of safety guidelines that are easy to follow. The rules of safety for woodworking are meant to be easy to remember, and are generally used to guide common sense. However, failure to adhere to the safety rules could cause serious injuries. The workplace isn't destined to a life of leisure. It's time to learn and adopt high-quality practices of safety , which can make working with timber more enjoyable and enjoyable.

1. Also, wear safety gear.
It may appear to be an unwritten rule of common sense but it's essential to keep in mind. A hat with ear protection can be an advantage when using of loud authority tools such as routers and surface planes. Wear a wax mitt when the finishes are being applied. Always wear your protective glasses. Once you are in the market this will be the first thing you'll need.

2. Dress in appropriate clothes

The reason you should wear loose or baggy clothing is the high chance that they could be caught by the blade or cutting head. Therefore, you should ensure that you wear clothes that will make you more suitable to the working environment however, you must also be aware of your own. Be sure to take off any jewelry that is dangerous or metallic items like bracelets or chains prior to beginning work.

3. Avoid using anything that may affect your response time or judgment

It's the same as driving an automobile: To prevent accidents, it is important to stay clear of cabinet of alcohol and drugs. The dangers in the woodshop are much higher when you use the wrong tool in a rash manner, or when you're inexperienced to know the right thing to do. Don't mix drinking and function even if it's one or two drinks.

4. Turn off Control

When you're moving blades on power tools, try to turn off the source of power. As well as ensuring your switch has been turned turned off Make sure that the tool isn't powered by electricity as the switch could fail or be accidentally turned on.

5. Utilizing an ordinary Cable Extension

Utilizing one large job conservatory string to connect each of your tools that you are authorized to use. This will ensure that the power for every device is turned off. A lot of strings could become difficult to navigate and cause danger to fall.

6. Avoid using Bits and Blunt Blades

This may be obvious to realize how dangerous an extremely hefty wounding tool could be. These machines need to be ready to cut, and may be pushed back or attached in the process. Sharp bits and blades will ensure cleaner cuts.

7. For Metal check stock

Before you actually cut or creating a slash ensure that the stock doesn't already have screws, nails or any other metal parts buried within it. The spinning blades, nails and (and other pieces of metal) are not able to blend well at the same time, causing serious damage to the stockpile as well as the cutting head. This could cause the stock to return and result in damage, so ensure that your stock's safe (or using a metal radar to verify it's safe for you).

8. Make use of the blade

The majority of control equipment is designed to require the route that pieces of wood follows when using the process, which is reversed by the motion in the direction of the blade's head. This means you need to ensure that instead of causing it the router bit or blade cuts along with the wood's movement.

9. Never exceed the speed of a continuous cutter

Be patient and wait until the cutter's rotation stopping before it is able to remove the waste or cut-offs. Also, removing the misuse using shove sticks or a scrap pieces to ensure that an accidental power device knob malfunction doesn't cause death to be on the secure side.

10. Minimize divergences

If you trade in a manner that is interrupted it is important to ensure that you end your current task before focusing your attention to something else (final an slash, in particular working with the control tool).

4.2 FAMILIAR WOODWORKING TRAPES and methods to stay clear of them

It is a must to find a woodworker who hasn't ruined his work (or at least not done anything which caused him to conduct extensive study to repair it). If you take your time, you'll avoid making a number of errors entirely. The most common error timber workers are prone to is speeding too much. It's a race and you're ready to finish a task. Don't do it. It is not just possible to be more likely to sabotage your idea, but you could also end up damaging something more valuable to you. Accelerating too fast is the most common cause of injury at workshops. Here are some of the most frequent woodworking errors, as well as methods to avoid them or fix them altogether.

A rough or blotchy surface

Sometimes, blotchy finishes can be obtained with finish oil like stain or Danish oil, or. The finish can turn out to appear blotchy because the holes in certain timbers like crimson are filled various quantities of oil, and give an uneven appearance.

After the damage has been done, there is no way to fix it, so you need to be taking the time to plan for this prior to beginning working on. Two methods to avoid this from happening:

1. Make use of a abrade sealer or a similar product to fill in wood pores prior to the end is placed.

2. Make sure to use a polish that sits on the top of the grain instead of taking it off. Two sources include polish and shellac.

The drawers or doors that do not have a strong construction are

Nothing is more depressing than when you've finished working on a cabinet and attempt to slide through the drawer only to find that the cabinet is simply too big to withstand the sludge. Do not remain in a state of confusion as to why this happens. You've made the plans in the first place, so why not?

The problem is that you've followed the blueprints. This is the scenario In the beginning, when you make a carcass for a cabinet the dimensions here and there may be different by 1/33 inch. If you try to put the carcass together, small differences can result in the overall dimensions that your cabinet is not strong enough.

The answer is simple to stay on until the carcass is finished and ready to build the drawers or doors. Then the elements that are listed on the plan are not considered and the body itself is put to work. What is the best way to ensure that the dimensions of the drawer or door match those of the body?

Stain not to be able to get

The most common reasons why a stain isn't able to be achieved is because you've worn the stuffing for your timber that blocks staining, or include a piece of wood that you did not clean completely after the piece was assemble.

These issues can be avoided, but aren't as easy to resolve. Therefore, ensure that you use wood stuffing, which is prone to getting marks and then clean all stick that leaks when you remove it from the joint. If you decide to apply a the stain of stainless to your walls, apply a color-changing glaze to the unstained area by changing the color and thickness until you are able to match the wood smudge. Allow it to dry, and then apply a topcoat.

Sanding that causes the wood bubbling

Certain woods, such as Birch, can become hairy if you polish too often on them. The wood breaks fibers, and creates hairy feathers on the wood's surface. This is why you shouldn't want to coat or stain the wood.

Joints that don't work

There's a huge need to create tight joints, however it isn't moving when you put the stick in and try to drag the joint in tandem. In addition, you have tight joints or only partially drag the joint at a time and experience "lock-up."

Make sure to dry fit your joints first, to avoid joints that are too firm. If you need to hit (or simply hit lightly) the joint using an hammer, then it is necessary to ease the joint prior to applying adhesive. If the joint is a Tenon and overlap slightly, you can cut down the tenon to pull the joint by tapping or hand.

Common WOODWORKING PITFALLS and HOW to stay clear of them
It would be difficult to find any woodworker who did not experience something unexpected that destroyed his work (or at least something that made him perform an enormous amount of work in order to fix it). Here are a few of the most frequent mistakes made by carpenters and methods of fixing the damage or stopping them.

The majority of mistakes can be avoided by slowing down. Haste is one of the most frequently encountered woodworkers' issue. It is easy to be stressed and want to finish an assignment. Don't do it. Don't do it. Not only are you more likely to endanger your work however, you may also endanger an even more significant thing - - yourself. The leading reason for workplace accidents is speeding.

If you find yourself wanting to rush things, stop and remember that rushing can cost you more in the long run , if you have to fix an error or visit an emergency department.

Uneven or BLOTCHY A FINISH

There are times when you see tangled surfaces due to an oil finish such as Danish paint or oil. The finish can be blotchy because the pores of some species of trees, such as cherry, absorb different amounts of oil and appear rough.

There is no way to fix this issue until the damage is already done Therefore, you must be sure to prepare the project beforehand. This issue can be solved by two ways:

Applying a sanding sealing agent or

another pores to fill in the wood pores prior to the final filling is put on.
Applying a polish to the it's surface, instead of absorption it. Two examples of this are shellac and varnish.

DOORS OR DRAWERS THAT DON'T DO NOT

There is nothing more painful than finishing the cabinet and getting ready to glue the drawer onto the cabinet, only to have it come to the end only to discover that the drawer isn't wide to accommodate the opening. Do not get caught up in the mess and wonder why this took place. You followed the plan in the end, so why not?

The issue is the fact that you've not been following the plans. This is the scenario When you build an adobe cabinet that is not properly measured, the measurements, here and there, as an example could be off in 1/32 inch. When you attempt to join the carcass tiny differences can cause your drawer to not be in line.

The answer is straightforward Wait until the doors or drawers are fully finished following the carcass has been removed. Don't forget about the size of the design and the function that came from the carcass. This means that the measurements of your door or drawer correspond to the dimensions from the carcass.

A TABLE That is ROCKS

Most of the time it is the case that after you've finished building the table, it wobbles. (It may not be recognized however, the fact that a majority of woodworkers have experienced the same experience.)

To prevent this from happening, make sure each leg is cut to in the exact same size. Place them in a jig for cutting panels and run them all at once on the table saw. It is important to make sure that when you glue the saw up, you'll get your table's square. Make the table leg/rail combination by two stages: first put the rails that are shorter into the legs. Then, insert the two pieces into long rails , after giving them the chance to completely dry. You should look for squares both ways -on upper part of the mounting as well as across the leg from lower to other side that of the head.

Make sure to square the table from the beginning. There may be issues that may occur. To repair the wobbly table following glueing, adjust the length of the leg until it's even. Set it on a bench to determine which leg has the most length. Begin by pushing the table towards the bench on this long leg. Moving the leg in a tight direction towards the bench's edge, then smooth the table surface. When this happens, if it is the longer leg the tabletop will spread out slightly. Utilizing a knife, you can draw a line where the bench's top is crossed by the leg of the table. To cut the leg down to the same level, you can make use of a sander, or a plane.

STAIN THAT CAN'T Take

The most frequent reasons not to use an oil stain is because you've employed a wood filler that isn't filled or contains glue that you did not completely clean off after installing the piece.

Both issues are simple to avoid, but simple to fix. Therefore, make sure you have the right wood filler to absorb stain and remove all glue that dribbles off a joint once it is put together.

If your project results in non-tuned areas, apply the coloured glaze (semi-transparent solution that is similar to stains or thin paints) on the surface that is not tuned

Change the colour and cover until it matches the wood stained. Dry it, and then cover the surface.

SANDING THAT MAKES WOOD Fuzzy

Many trees, such as birch, soften when you oversand. The wood fibres split and cause a gritty flush on the wood's surface. In this state you shouldn't stain or topcoat the wood.

If the wood is very soft, work down one or two grains of sandpaper (120 gr is a good starting point) and then sand the rest out. The only way to stop the soft wood is to ensure that you're not sanding over 150 grams of paper. However, you shouldn't use a scraper.

JOINTS THAT DO NOT FIT

You've done your best to make your joints close however, it doesn't work when you apply your glue and attempt to join them. It could be that you have too close joints or the joints only partially join and are locked up.'

Additionally, you should dry the joints first to avoid overly tight joints. If you are required to press (or tap) the joints using a briefcase, it is recommended to loosen the joints prior applying glue. Reduce the tenon's thickness in the case of mortise and Tenon. Then, you pull them using your hands or by tapping.

If you are locking the joints, you need to tap them very hard before clamping it once more before driving. It's impossible to force it to open in the event that you have locked the joint. Make sure to stop a joint that is locked first, which is as easy as joining the joint fully before you install it. Avoid the temptation to connect the joint only partially. Additionally, connect the joint prior to changing to a different joint.

TABLETOPS THAT DON'T FIT

After you've made the effort to select the right, fry and place on tables, you unhook the clamps and discover that the tabletop isn't smooth. There are two possible answers to your question If your wood wasn't bent, cupped or twist. The edges of the boards were not straight enough or the clamping pressure was too strong as the boards were put together.

Be sure to use the right joiner to produce perfect square edged edges to the boards to avoid this type of issue. Do not press the clamps too hard that the board begins falling off the clamps. An additional lock placed on the top of the boards could assist.

You'll need to plane it and sand down the surface to smooth a tabletop that is irregular. There is a loss of thickness to the wall and perhaps you do not want to proceed in this direction. The only option is to remove the joint's top and then restart. Relax It's not as difficult as it sounds and is much more straightforward to flatten with the help of a sander and a plane.

After the boards are removed, then attach them to ensure they have straight edges, sturdy edge joints , and then test them to be flatness. Then, force them to put the boards in a way that gives them enough force.

Wood that splits when being CUT
The motion of a wood piece through a saw could cause the blade spinning to crack due to the fragile edges of wood after the piece of wood leaves the saw. The tears are triggered on the back of boards when you cut grass.

A way to stop tears is to place the back edge of the wood before it is cut. The back wall is used as a frame to sacrifice the tear. Even if you have a rip as well as cutting surface, consider making the first and second rips cross-cutting. It is unlikely that the blade could break when cutting a rip and you don't have to consider a backup wall.

Joints that are too loose
A joint is often fitted too loosely. It is a major issue for mortise and tenon joints since their strength is contingent on the tightness of the mortise and Tenon. What can to do when the tenon that is in the mortise is loose? In addition to creating a new one it's a lot of adhesive that fills in the gaps. Standard wood glue carpenters won't work. It is necessary to use an epoxy adhesive, which is a two-part glue that can be growing to fill in gaps in wood.
Another option is to put the wood to the tenon, and cut it in order to fit the mortise.

Conclusion

Many people picture the blacksmith as someone who lived during a time gone by. They may be thinking of a medieval monk who hammered metal into horseshoes and swords. Blacksmithing isn't just a dying craft. Actually, the art blacksmithing has grown to be more popular that ever.

It was only a few months ago that I attended an arts & crafts festival in Shipshewana. In this big blacksmith shop, budding blacksmiths came from all over the region to show off their ability to strike an axe. You could find those who were experts in old weaponry, like swords and knives, as well those who made simple tools for home decor like this book.

It didn't matter the subject, creation was still beautiful. And that's what this book is all about. The projects you will find here are extremely flexible. It was made this way in order to allow you to discover what works best.

This book is designed to help both the experienced blacksmith and the novice. So with that out of the way, I hope this book has informed and motivated you to get on board the blacksmith train. DIY blacksmithing has never looked better. We are so grateful that you read!

www.ingramcontent.com/pod-product-compliance
Lightning Source LLC
Chambersburg PA
CBHW050026130526
44590CB00042B/1926